CORSAGE FEATURING JAPANESE
FUJI CHRYSANTHEMUMS

Champagne colored Fuji chrysanthemums dominate this corsage, but other types are introduced for variety of form and interest through petal texture. The bronze-green ribbon deepens the color effect as it appears in small areas around the periphery. (Both corsages by Glad Reusch.)

CORSAGE FEATURING THE EXOTIC
GLORIOSA SUPERBA LILY

The colors of this climbing lily glow from warm orange-red through the neighboring hues of yellow, yellow-green, and green. Curling lines of the flowers guide the eye toward the rhythmic center of green. A glossy, chartreuse satin bow with blue-green lining carries on the color analogy.

CORSAGE CRAFT

by

GLAD REUSCH

AND

MARY NOBLE

SKETCHES BY GLAD REUSCH

SECOND EDITION

D. VAN NOSTRAND COMPANY, INC.

PRINCETON, NEW JERSEY

TORONTO   LONDON

Van Nostrand Regional Offices: *New York, Chicago, San Francisco*

D. Van Nostrand Company, Ltd., *London*

D. Van Nostrand Company (Canada), Ltd., *Toronto*

Library of Congress Catalog Card No. 60-10290

04674b20
PRINTED IN THE UNITED STATES OF AMERICA

This volume is dedicated to the corsage students of the Garden Clubs of Jacksonville and St. Petersburg, Florida, and the Washington State Federation of Garden Clubs, whose enthusiasm kindled the inspiration.

Preface to Second Edition

Corsage craft is the art of using flowers for personal adornment. It is a fascinating form of the encompassing art of flower arranging.

Corsage making was a craft little known and understood by the home gardener until this book was published in 1951. Since then several other volumes on the subject have appeared, garden clubs have taught the art to their members and to junior gardeners, and the National Corsage Club has provided information to its thousands of members. Now corsages have a place in every flower show, and specialized shows for corsages and fashions are exciting events.

Our purpose is to show you how to use your flowers for your own enjoyment. In the study of flower arranging you have learned how to display your blooms in your home. We want you to wear them, too, to show them off when you go out. To do this best, you must fashion them into artistic corsages.

When our first edition appeared, there were few home greenhouses. Now small greenhouses are important features of many home gardens and the exotics described in our chapter "Beyond the Garden Gate" are frequently home grown. If your hobby is orchids, anthuriums or amaryllis, you will want to display your prize blooms in corsages by wearing them on special occasions.

But any kind of flower, from the lowliest zinnia to the rarest vanda can be used for a corsage. Both types challenge the imagination of the designer.

We hope that you will derive great pleasure from working with your flowers. You may make simple designs if you are a beginner in corsage craft, and progress to the more complicated techniques as you master the steps in preparation and assembling.

We hope, too, that you will coordinate your flowers with your costumes . . . and plan your wardrobe and your garden with your corsages in mind. We hope you will enter the corsage classes in your local flower shows and take many blue ribbons. Most of all we hope you will have more fun with your flowers because of your mastery of corsage craft.

January 1960   GLAD REUSCH
                                                  MARY NOBLE

Photo credits:
James N. Keen, Plates I, II, III, IV, VII, VIII, IX, X, XII, XIII, XIV, XV, XVI, XVII, XXIII
W. Burton Talbott, Plate V
Broadway Portrait Studio, Plate XI
Joyce Wright, Plates VI, XVIII, XIX, XXI, XXIV, XXV, XXVI
Mary Noble, Plates XX, XXII
Lou Egner, Jacket photo of Miss Noble
Bernie Oram, Cover and Frontispiece
St. Petersburg Times, Jacket photo of Mrs. Reusch

CONTENTS

vii

FOREWORD

To wear a corsage is to indicate that there is an occasion. Not only does a corsage add a festive atmosphere but it also gives an air of importance. The choice of flowers, of colors, and design have significance when a corsage has been chosen or made especially for you and just to please you. What a wonderful way to express hospitality, appreciation, or admiration.

Something gay and friendly occurs when a corsage box or bag is placed in your hand. How many times have we heard the happy question, "Oh, is this for *me?*" The excitement of opening the box, the pleasure of wearing the corsage, and the compliments and comments of friends add to the joy of the recipient—the fortunate one.

Many kinds of satisfaction enter into this project of corsage-making and giving. The craft can be a possible means of support; a comfort to the aged and ill; a means of recreation for our juniors and teenagers. And always the pleasure of doing for others makes corsage craft worthwhile. This art we can encourage with the knowledge that it does only good and adds to happiness in this world of today. I extend best wishes for the continued success of *Corsage Craft* by Glad Reusch and Mary Noble.

HAZEL JOHNSON
(Mrs. Jamie Johnson)
President, National Council of State
Garden Clubs, Inc.

I

WHAT IS CORSAGE CRAFT?

Flower-wearing has been a custom through the ages of history. Present-day corsages follow in the traditions of the Grecian garland, the Oriental hair arrangement, the Hawaiian lei, and the Colonial tussie-mussie. But to these designs, the modern art of corsage craft adds the knowledge of conditioning the flowers to preserve their freshness, assembling techniques to hold the designs secure, and additional arrangements in harmony with the fashions of the day.

The art of flower arrangement for home decoration and flower show exhibition has been taught for years. Now the allied art of making corsages is coming to the fore; and more and more garden clubs, home demonstration groups, and high school organizations are seeking information and instruction. Classifications for corsages are now included in most flower show schedules.

Every gardener wants to display her prize blooms, and what better way is there than by wearing them in a corsage? Fresh flowers give a lift that is equaled only by a new hat. Although most people can't have a new hat every day, they can have a fresh corsage. Once the habit of wearing fresh flowers every day has been established, your garden and wardrobe can be planned simultaneously, so that corsages and costumes will be harmonious. For a corsage is not an extra decoration—properly planned, *it is a floral accessory* that is a definite part of the costume.

When Glad Reusch (pronounced Roy-sh) was Director of the Garden Center in Jacksonville, Florida, she taught her corsage art to the club members. Their enjoyment of this new hobby was so wholehearted that it became apparent that a book was needed, making the information available to gardeners everywhere. Nine of the photographs included here are of designs made by Mrs. Reusch's Jacksonville students.

A corsage need not be five rosebuds, some fern, and a silver bow. Instead, we advocate using a variety of flowers and foliage from the garden. Zinnias, ivy leaves, holly berries, and pine cones all have a place in corsages, and the garden offers a challenge to experiment with other new material.

There are many ways to wire, tape, and arrange flowers in corsages. Artists, florists, and flowers differ. We give you, in the following chapters, the technique Glad Reusch has practiced for years. Although many flowers and designs are included, the possibilities are endless. The hobbyist who masters these techniques will be able to adapt them to any flower, for the methods given here cover all types of wiring, from preparing a single camellia so the head won't fall off, to the construction of an intricate bridal bouquet. Although most of the materials mentioned are generally available, some are favorites of East Coast, others are known only in the West, and still others are restricted to the Deep South. Yet the way of handling these various items may be adapted to similar forms in any climate. Once the techniques are understood, the designer can assemble any plant material into her own beautiful designs. The technique for preparing exotics produced by the greenhouse gardener is here, too, and Chapter IX tells you what to use for material when the garden is snowbound.

Making corsages is not only a hobby for gardeners, though most of the flowers and greens suggested are found in home gardens. It is also a hobby for the teen-age girl who makes her own party corsages, and for mothers whose sons want corsages for their Saturday-night dates. The apartment dweller can join in, too, by selecting flowers from the corner flower stand or neighborhood florist.

Likewise, a corsage is more than a costume accessory. It is a wonderful gift. Pinned to the patient's pillow, it is more tangible than a vase of flowers across the room. Atop a gift box or as a party favor, or as an expression of friendship, a corsage is always appropriate.

A word about wearing flowers is in order. Flowers should be worn as they grow, heads up and stems down. Pin the corsage securely, so it doesn't wobble and does feel comfortable. If you plan to dance, choose an out-of-the-way design. This could be a conventional hair arrangement, a pony tail circlet, a diadem across the forehead, a wristlet or a pair of glamorous floral earrings. Choose designs that are in line with the fashions of the day, and flowers that are harmonious with your clothes and your personality, and your corsages will add immeasurably to your appearance and pleasure!

PLATE I

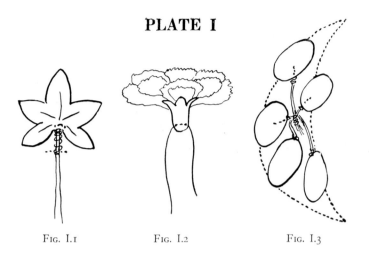

FIG. I.1   FIG. I.2   FIG. I.3

Material: White carnations, silvered ivy leaves.

Form: Crescent.

Line: Two intertwined crescents—silver curve and white curve.

Color harmony: All white with a moonlight glow of silver.

Texture: Frilly carnations are set off by smooth, glistening ivy leaves.

Finishing: Horizontally lined silver ribbon, used for accent, adds a
third textural variety.

Technique:

Using ivy leaves of different sizes, paint heavily on both sides with
aluminum paint and wire through the base as shown in Fig. I.1.

Pull back the green calyx of each carnation halfway to allow the
flower to fluff out. Remove stem completely. Push a 24-gauge wire
through the calyx horizontally (Fig. I.2). Pull ends down vertically.
Twist one wire around the other close up under the flower and cover
with white floral tape.

Assemble the five wired carnations and eleven leaves as shown in
the skeleton, Fig. I.3. Arrange so the eye will follow the silver from
the two top leaves to the lower tip, with the bulk of the leaves dominating the focal point.

Make a bow of several long loops and tie securely around corsage
at assembly point. Arrange loops so that they drape softly from the
center of interest. Cut surplus wires off short on a slant.

Corsage by: Mrs. J. C. Sterchi.

4

PLATE I

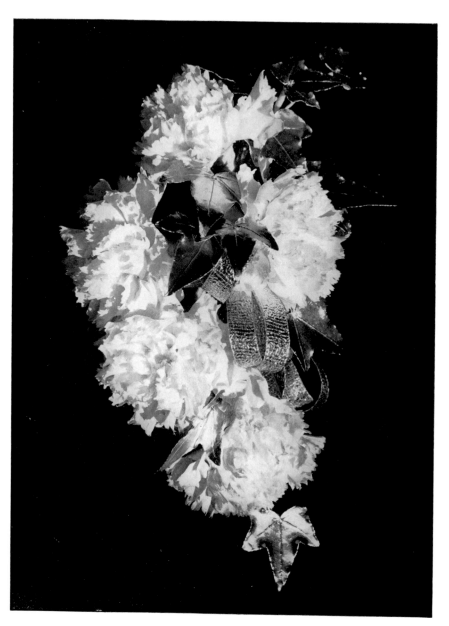

Crescent of White Carnations with Silvered Ivy Leaves

II

DESIGN

In designing a corsage there are three basic factors to consider: (a) the flowers available, (b) the costume, and (c) the occasion. It is much the same as deciding whether to wear a small tailored hat or a big straw with a veil. The corsage, too, must look as though it *belongs,* for it is as much a costume accessory as the hat.

After you have decided which dress to wear, go to the garden and select flowers and foliages that harmonize with it. Then sit at your worktable and experiment until you work out a design that is in keeping with the flowers, the costume, and the occasion. Hang the dress you plan to wear near the worktable and hold the corsage up to it as you progress with the design. The effect will guide you in adding or discarding material.

The elements of design in corsage craft are the same as those you apply, consciously or unconsciously, in dressmaking, flower arrangement, or interior decoration.

Form

Since making a corsage is not just putting together a few posies and tying them with a piece of ribbon, but a careful arrangement of harmonious parts, you may well begin the design with a definite form in mind.

The form is the silhouette of the finished product, the imaginary line around the outer edges of the corsage. It is the shape of the corsage. The form may be based on the curved line (circle, crescent, and Hogarth curve) or the straight line (triangle, square, and rectangle).

A *round* corsage (Fig. 1) is the nosegay form. Three geraniums surrounded by geranium foliage make an attractive round corsage for daytime wear. If the ring style with an open center is desired, try violets, miniature pansies, or florets of narcissus wired end to end. The glamellia corsage (Plate VI) and the holly corsage (Plate XI) illustrate the round form.

The chrysanthemum corsage (Plate VII) is in the *crescent* form (Fig. 2). The crescent may also be made up with flowers in three stages of bloom with open blossoms in the center and half-open and tight buds on the ends. The crescent form using flowers in gradation is especially effective when chosen for camellias.

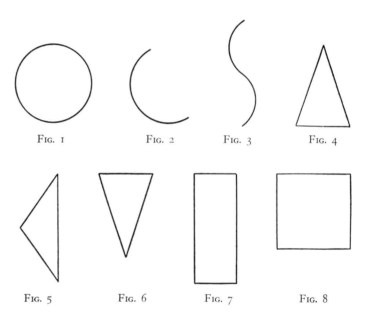

FIG. 1   FIG. 2   FIG. 3   FIG. 4

FIG. 5   FIG. 6   FIG. 7   FIG. 8

The *Hogarth* "line of beauty" (Fig. 3) is in the shape of an "S," a reversed "S," or variations. Like the crescent, the Hogarth generally works out best with the weight in the center and the buds on the ends, but it may be effectively used with open blossoms at the top and buds trailing down the curve. Anemones are effective in the Hogarth form. See the orchid corsage (Plate XVI) for the use of one large flower and several smaller ones in the Hogarth form.

The spray type corsage is generally based on the *triangle* (Fig. 4). Daffodils may be successfully used in the triangle with buds for the points. The daylily and calendula corsage (Plate II in this chapter) is a triangular corsage, as is the one of wood roses (Plate X).

Blue cornflowers and yellow marguerites lend themselves to a long triangle (Fig. 5).

When the broad part of the triangle is at the top, in jabot style (Fig. 6), white Esther Reed daisies may be arranged across the top and large freesias used to fill in the lower section.

The *rectangular* form (Fig. 7) is used for a long shoulder corsage. Two full carnations and six smaller ones (of divided carnations) filled out with silver ribbon are adaptable to the rectangular form.

The *square* form (Fig. 8) is frequently used for other than shoulder corsages, though the foliage corsage (Plate III) is in the square form with an added point at the top. A black ribbon necklace, lavaliere length with matching pendant ribbon loops, can be centered with a minute square corsage made of one small open rose snugly surrounded by hyacinth bells.

Form also means the outlines of the individual flowers and leaves used in the corsage. A corsage need not be confined to material of a single form, but the combination should be pleasing. In the corsage shown in Plate II, round calendulas, star-shaped daylilies, and rectangular buds are used together to advantage. In Plate III, triangular ivy leaves, round clover blossoms, and gently curved pittosporum leaves are harmonious.

LINE

Line is not only the outline form but also the grouping of the skeleton lines that make up the composition. The beauty of the design depends in a large measure on the proper placement of the main line and the subordinate lines. Each line must be important to the other lines and to the composition as a whole. Each and every line should lead to the focal point of the corsage, the one center of interest in the design.

Careful study of the corsage "skeletons" accompanying the plates throughout the book will give an understanding of the lines applied in corsage craft. The curved line within the triangular form may be

seen in Plate II, for the eye quickly follows in a crescent from the top
buds to the curved stem endings.

COLOR

The color of the flowers you wear is a very personal matter of emo-
tional importance. Your flowers should harmonize with your personality and mood as much as with your costume.

A review of some of the simple harmonies will be of interest and help
in planning the corsage. Any color wheel is satisfactory for planning
harmonies. The one shown is a 12-segment wheel based on pigment
color. In working with colors, it is advisable to think of the general
blending of the colors, as in a rainbow, rather than sharply defined
separations shown in the segments of the color wheel.

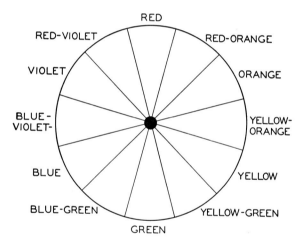

Red is found at the top of the color wheel. The color opposite is green
and here we have a simple *complementary* or contrasting harmony.
The red color can be lightened with white and it becomes pink. The
strong green can be reduced to a light tint of green. Any opposite colors
form complementary harmonies. In corsage craft, a complementary
harmony is represented by red carnations with green ribbon or green
foliage. Similarly, a pink rose and an apple-green ribbon contrast pleas-
ingly. If the colors are kept near the same value (the light or dark of
the color) the harmony is considered a little more acceptable.

An *analogous* harmony is made up of neighboring colors: yellow, yellow-green, green, and blue-green. Plate III shows a corsage made of analogous (neighboring) colors: creamy-white clover, yellow-green pittosporum leaves, blue-green ivy, green ribbon, and stems. The day-lily and calendula corsage in Plate II is a simple analogy of yellow and brown. The buds are a soft creamy-yellow, the daylilies a sulphur yellow, and the calendulas a deep yellow. The rich brown calendula centers are emphasized by the use of brown ribbon.

Monochromatic means a one-color harmony in which tints and shades of one color are employed. These may run from the lightest tint, almost white, to the deepest shade, just so the color remains in the same segment of the color wheel. For a blush, pink, rose, and maroon combination use light pink button chrysanthemums, one large rose chrysanthemum, fruit of the Eleyi crabapple, and deep rosy photinia foliage.

Triadic color is a fascinating harmony made up of three colors at equal distances around the color wheel. If the three points of an equilateral triangle touch the edge of the color circle, the contacted colors form a perfect triadic harmony. In the 12-color chart, this means every fourth color: red, yellow, and blue. A shift of one segment to the right results in a harmony of red orange, yellow-green, and blue-violet. In selecting flowers to represent the triadic color scheme, choose one color for the dominating note, a smaller amount of color for the second, and a tiny touch of color for the third. Equal amounts of color in a design are rarely desirable and seldom satisfying.

The four-color scheme, *tetradic* color, is easily discovered on the color wheel if, instead of a triangle used for triadic color, you cut a square that will touch the edges of the color circle. At the point where each of these corners touches the circle is found a color making up the tetradic harmony. Example: red, yellow-orange, green, and blue-violet. Shift the square one segment to the right and the tetradic harmony will be red-orange, yellow, blue-green, and violet. Skill in the use of grayed tones and shades facilitates the tetradic color scheme.

When making a corsage that is to be worn at night, it is advisable to look at the flowers you plan to use under artificial light the night before. Some of the colors that are lovely in the daytime lose their effectiveness at night. For instance, blues and dark purples are tricky under artificial light. Orchid tones are more effective if a red-violet coloring is present. Yellow loses its identity at night, but white, pink, and rose are beautiful under artificial light.

Texture

Texture is a surface quality. Consider the texture of the flowers, the foliage, and the ribbon for harmony or for interesting contrast. Consider also the appropriateness of the background. You would not wear a corsage of delicate flowers on a heavy tweed suit any more than you would choose a denim blouse to go with a satin skirt.

Flower petals have surfaces that are tender, fragile, ruffled, waxy, glossy, and woolly. Berries or fruit may be shiny, dull, plushy, and pebbly. Ribbon textures are easily separated into dull, smooth, glossy, coarse, or fine. The prize-winning corsage is often chosen because of its excellent textural quality. An especially satisfying combination of textures highlights the tailored corsage in Plate III. The soft petaled clover forms and the delicate roseate pittosporum leaves are emphasized by the smooth broad surfaces of the ivy leaves and the smooth taffeta ribbon. Another note of distinction in this corsage is the use of common material in an uncommon manner.

Proportion and Balance

Proportion and balance are of paramount importance in corsage design.

Proportion is the relation of the parts of the corsage to the whole. The forms and colors must be considered. Usually the larger blossoms are found in the center of the design to make the focal point, and the smaller blossoms at the edges of the form. Likewise with color. Many light colored flowers will be needed to balance one or two visually heavier darker flowers, and here again the lighter tones are usually on the outer edges of the form.

The size of the corsage in relation to the size of the wearer is most important. A tiny flower jewel is ineffective on a size 40 shoulder, while someone petite staggers under a shoulder spray of hibiscus. The occasion also affects the size. A smart tailored corsage for daytime wear is smaller and more compact than a loose spray corsage for evening wear.

Balance is the weight that is found on each side of the imaginary line down the center of the design. Both symmetrical and asymmetrical balance are applied to corsage design. In symmetrical balance, the same composition is found on both sides of the imaginary axis. (See the corsage of roses and stock in Plate XV.) In asymmetrical balance, the parts vary on each side of the axis but the visual weight balances. For example, an imaginary line down the center of the corsage in Plate II gives two daylily-calendulas and four buds on one side and only one daylily-calendula and the ribbon on the other side. However, the dark brown ribbon weighs more heavily than the light yellow flowers, and balances the composition.

Proportion and balance can be achieved by experimenting with the lines, forms, and colors until the design is pleasing to the eye. This is called pictorial balance.

Contrasts of light and dark in color, of coarse and fine in texture, of simple and complex in form add zest to any design. The elements of design discussed here are basic principles to be applied and experimented with by the designer. A mellowness and harmony can be felt when the design is satisfying.

The beginner in corsage craft should first start with the simple lines, forms, and color harmonies. Practice in design will bring confidence that will lead to experiments in the more complex combinations of the design elements. The eye is the best judge. If the finished corsage is pleasing, the design is good.

PLATE II

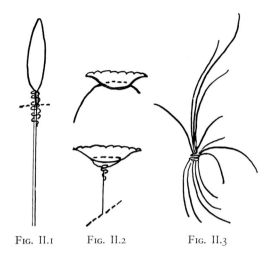

FIG. II.1   FIG. II.2   FIG. II.3

Material: Daylilies, daylily buds, calendulas.
Form: Triangle.
Line: Crescent within the triangle.
Color harmony: Analogous—yellow and brown.
Texture: Waxy daylilies, frilly calendulas, shiny and dull ribbon.
Finishing: Curved stem endings covered with white floral tape. Brown
    satin ribbon and brown taffeta ribbon.
Technique:

Cut stems of daylily buds to ½ inch. Wire tightly by twisting the
center of a 14-inch length of 26-gauge wire around the stem several
times. Straighten both ends of the wire and cover with floral tape
(Fig. II.1).

Remove calendula stem and insert a wisp of moist cotton at the
base of the flower. Push a short piece of 26-gauge wire through the
lower calyx, wrap one end around the other under the flower, and
cut end on a slant so it will pierce the lily trumpet easily (Fig. II.2).

Remove stamen and pistil of daylily. Insert calendula into trumpet
of lily and tape trumpet. Push an 18-inch length of wire through tape,
trumpet, and base of calendula, then straighten ends to form a double wire stem. Cover wires completely, beginning where wire pierced
trumpet.

14

PLATE II

Triangle of Daylilies with Buds and Calendulas

Assemble the wired flowers and buds as shown in the skeleton. (Fig. II.3). Bind tightly at assembly point and cover assembling wire with tape. Note the spacing. Each flower has its distinct sphere of influence without crowding. Fill the void on the left side of the skeleton with bow made of brown satin and taffeta ribbon, completing the pictorial balance. Tie the bow first and then tie the ends around the corsage at the assembly point. Curve stem endings gently to balance buds at top of composition.

Corsage by: Mrs. George Mason.

III

GROWING AND CONDITIONING THE MATERIAL

The first step in planning the corsage is the choice of plants for your garden. Planting for continuous bloom will provide material for all seasons, and special treatment will induce some plants to produce flowers for an extended period. For instance, early spring bulbs put in the ground at two-week intervals will provide flowers for a longer time than if they are planted all at once. On plants such as delphinium, larkspur, zinnia, and Canterbury bells, the laterals may be forced into bloom by cutting the central spike and fertilizing the roots. Houseplants for winter bloom in cold climates may be selected with corsages in mind. Many decorative potplants will tolerate living-room conditions, and most bulbs can be brought to bloom indoors. Even some orchids will flourish on the windowsill. If a small greenhouse is available, there is almost no limit to your choice of plants.

Flowering shrubs and trees provide many blossoms suitable for corsages and can be chosen to harmonize with your landscape scheme as well as your favorite corsage designs. Consider also the possibilities of berried shrubs and plants with unusual foliage characteristics. If your garden is bare at certain times, take note of the neighbors' suitable blooms and plan to include them next year.

Early spring favorites are daffodil, narcissus, hyacinth, tulip, lily of the valley, crocus, freesia, tuberose, and Siberian iris. In summer, use Dutch iris, watsonia, gladiolus, gloriosa, anemone, and calla. Fall and winter materials are determined by the climate. The tropical and subtropical gardens offer fresh flowers the year round, while gardeners in cold regions have an unlimited amount of material on which to draw, as discussed in Chapter IX, "Corsages Without Flowers."

Some of the "musts" among annuals and perennials are calendula, carnation, chrysanthemum, delphinium, fuchsia, primrose, rose, snapdragon, verbena, and zinnia.

Neither your own fence nor your state line need be a limitation to the materials you use in your corsages. Exchanging cones, seedpods, and other dried materials with friends in other sections of the country adds to the fascination of the corsage hobby. Items that are commonplace in one state are considered exotic in another. Cotton pods from the South are exchanged for eucalyptus pods from the West Coast; bittersweet and bayberries go to the desert from New England; madrona berries and snowberries from Washington add glamour to a Florida corsage. Galax leaves from North Carolina are nationwide favorites, and the unusual wood roses from Hawaii cause a sensation on the mainland.

CULTURE

Strange as it may seem, the actual preparation for the final cutting of corsage flowers begins with the proper soil conditions. If you would have flowers last well, they must be grown well. The good gardener ascertains the soil, food, and moisture requirements of her plants, and caters to their individual needs. And in reverse, the garden's prize blooms can best be displayed in attractive corsages.

PICKING THE FLOWERS

Conditioning the flowers prior to making them into the corsage largely determines the length of their life. Proper treatment when picking will add immeasurably to their stamina. Since conditioning of most flowers calls for overnight soaking, plan the corsage and pick the flowers the day before it is to be worn.

Flowers for corsage use should be gathered before sunup or after sundown. Use a sharp knife or sharp scissors. Cut the stems on a slant. Select flowers in three stages of development—bud, half-open, and full-blown. This variety of form adds interest to the design. Choose only the choicest and freshest blossoms available.

For most flowers it is advisable to put them in water immediately on cutting. Take a container into the garden with you. The ideal container for this purpose is a shallow pan fitted with a piece of hardware cloth having one-fourth-inch square mesh. Cut the flowers with 1-inch stems. Since this is the usual length for making into corsages, they are ready to be wired without recutting. Also, the short stems enable the flowers to take up water more rapidly than long stems. Place immediately in the container, putting the blossoms far enough apart in the mesh so the flower heads are not crowded. Allow the flowers to stay in the container overnight or for a comparable period. Place in a cool place away from drafts. Be sure the container is thoroughly clean before each use.

If long stems are preferred and some of the blossoms are to be used for arrangements, place flowers in a bucket of water up to their necks. Strip the leaves from the lower third of the stems to prevent bacterial decay and unpleasant odor. Cyclamen, narcissus, calla, and some of the other bulb flowers will last longer if the entire stem is pulled from the bulb.

When using gladiolus, delphinium, stock, or hyacinth blooms, pinch off only the lower florets and allow the spikes to continue developing for future use.

Preservatives

The best insurance for longevity of a corsage flower is to pick only fresh blossoms. A flower that is picked as soon as it is unfurled may be expected to last a reasonable time. Aspirin and floral powders add a little life to declining blossoms, but if the flower has been open on the stalk for two or three days, its life will be short no matter what steps are taken to prolong it. The fleeting flowers, such as cosmos, crape myrtle, tigridia, poppy, and clematis are seldom used for corsages. However, queen crape myrtle holds up well for jewelry.

More than three-fourths of the flowers you use for corsage work can be suitably conditioned by the long-drink procedure described above. However, a few corsage favorites require special treatment.

The poor-keepers such as the Christmas rose (*Helleborus niger*), and alyssum should be completely plunged in cool water.

All woody stems—chrysanthemums, roses, and flowering shrubs—should be crushed or pounded for 2 inches to facilitate the intake of water.

Dogwood, flowering cherry, and other tree branches are aided by peeling back the lower bark and cutting up into the stem crisscross.

When the stem bleeds (poinsettia, dahlia, euphorbia, and forgetme-not) it is necessary to place the end in an inch of boiling water for about two minutes. First cover the flowers with a newspaper funnel to protect them from the steam. Searing the end with a gas flame or match serves the same purpose.

Lilacs will stay fresh longer if the uppermost leaf remains.

Lilies should have the pollen removed to prolong the life of the flowers and because it stains the costume.

Gardenias drink through their petals; hence placing the blossoms under a moist cotton covering in an airtight box will add to their durability. Or, cover them with facial tissues lightly sprinkled.

Waterlilies should be picked the first day they open to insure long life. If this is impractical, warm paraffin dropped into the center will force the petals to stay open after dark.

To keep some varieties of camellias from losing their heads, drop candle wax over the calyx, using a color that matches the petals so wax will be inconspicuous. Or cover with dampened facial tissues.

Wrap maidenhair fern in damp newspapers.

Wrap yarn around the buds to delay the opening of roses.

For other specific details, consult the Appendix charts, where notes are made of such special treatment as the use of sugar, salt, oil of peppermint, ammonia, vinegar, and cloves for flower preservation. A wax preparation is available for preserving corsages and bouquets for sentimental reasons, but for wearing, flowers should be fresh.

If flowers have wilted and need reviving, recut the stems and place ends in a hot water bath and then immediately in a cold bath. If necessary, repeat the procedure a second time.

In choosing material for corsages, you will find your designs more exciting if you experiment with new material from the garden. However, in using a flower for the first time, it is well to test its keeping qualities before taking it out in public. It is most disappointing to wear a corsage out proudly, only to have it shatter or collapse. If necessary, make up a sample corsage a few days ahead of time and wear it around the house. When you know that your material will endure, you can wear your corsage with confidence.

Pre-treating Foliages

Foliages are conditioned much like flowers. In most instances, the leaf is sturdier than the flower, and the deep water bath for a few hours is sufficient. The richer and heavier the texture of the leaf, the less need for long soaking. Camellia, gardenia, rhododendron, croton, gladiolus, iris, spathyphyllum, huckleberry, loquat, skimmia, and salal belong to the sturdy group. Other leaves of soft texture, as maple, oak, dogwood, rose, and chrysanthemum, should have their stems hammered for about 2 inches and then be placed in cold water. Still others, coleus, geranium, funkia, dahlia, violet, peony, hydrangea, and lily of the valley, should remain in deep water for 12 hours, and may need a stem dip in boiling water also.

Leaves of shiny texture can stand actual washing or polishing. Soap and water, vegetable oil, furniture wax, or special foliage cleaners are suitable. A plastic spray is also usable.

If colored leaves are placed in half-water and half-glycerine solution for about two weeks, the color will remain almost indefinitely. Try this with dogwood and maple. Only about 1 inch of solution is needed, just enough to cover the stems. In the case of magnolia grandiflora, a handsome antique finish is acquired this way. Experiment with oak, rubber, photinia glabra and flowering quince leaves.

For an unusual effect, try skeletonizing leaves. Choose heavy green leaves, like magnolia. Dissolve ½ pint lye in 2 to 3 gallons water in a 5-gallon porcelain or enamel pan. Simmer for 1 hour. Turn leaves gently from top to bottom with blunt tongs. Then place on a board and brush ever so gently (preferably under slowly running water) until the solid portion is removed and only veins remain. Dry leaves between paper towels. To alter color, soak skeletonized leaves in chlorox or a color remover 2 to 3 hours. Rinse well and dry between paper towels. After leaves dry, color with a regular hot bath dye or a color tint suitable for fabrics. Skeletonized leaves are on the market as Angel Feathers. If not available in the desired color, buy white ones and tint them.

DYEING

Dyeing of flowers is generally frowned upon, but you may have to resort to dye when certain colors are needed and natural flowers in those colors are not available. Several types of dye may be used: liquid or spray flower dye, powder, ink, Tintex, powdered chalk, cold water paint, or calcimine. Of course, white flowers respond the best to dye, but some of the pastels are suitable.

To use a liquid dye, keep the flower out of water from the time it is picked. As soon as it becomes limp, place it in the dye bath and allow it to drink up the liquid. Flowers can soak up some types of dye through the stem, but must be "dunked" in other types and then rinsed in clear water. Follow directions on the container. Tintex is soaked through the stem. Dyeing may take from a few minutes to an hour and calls for experimentation. A Tintex bath is slower and may require 20 hours. Carnations, daffodils, daisies, sweet peas, and narcissi respond to liquid dye.

Heavier textured flowers such as callas and gardenias benefit from the powder treatment. Place a quantity of powder dye in a paper bag. Put the blossom head down in the bag, gather the top of the bag tightly around the stem, and shake well.

Place all stems of treated flowers in a cold bath immediately.

Dried grasses, seed pods, and cones may be brightened in color by the use of shellac mixed half and half with alcohol and painted or sprayed on materials. Metallic bronzing powders mixed with colored enamel may be used to change the color. The tropical cecropia leaf responds well to white shoe polish—the kind that does not rub off. For a pastel tint, add a little vegetable coloring or show-card paint. Use discretion in tinting dried materials as the natural color is generally more pleasing.

EQUIPMENT AND TOOLS

The essential materials used to make a corsage are wire and tape. Green corsage wire, coated to prevent rust, is available in several gauges. The four generally used are 32, 28, 26, and 24, reading from fine to coarse. Heavy 18 and 22 gauge wires are needed occasionally.

Stretchable floral tape for covering stems and wires comes under various trade names and is available in a number of colors. Green is best for general purposes, although white, brown, and the pastel shades are effective. Red tape is appropriate for Christmas corsages. Brown or black tape around the stems of flowers in hair designs for brunettes gives emphasis to blossoms; yellow or white tape may be used for blondes. Ribbon plays a glamorous role when needed for accent or harmony. Usual widths are $2\frac{7}{16}$th and $3\frac{5}{8}$ inches, but the ingenious designer will find use for widths from very narrow to very wide. The texture of the ribbon should be considered in relation to the texture of the flowers and the costume. Favorite ribbons come in satin, taffeta, lacey tinsel, velvet, and metallic weaves, and in an infinite color range from soft pastels to the rich deep tones of autumn. Two-toned ribbons, available in every color, blend, and contrast, add distinction.

Corsage accessories include chenille, gold and silver cord, colored tinseled wire, pigtail wire, metallic lace and velvet leaves, collarettes, cellophane bouquet holders, wrist bands, earring bases, fan frames, gardenia shields, net, maline, cellophane, and lace. Visit the trimming counter of your department store and revel in the wide choice of braids and other unusual materials. There is no limit to the possibilities that may be tried by the creative designer. Accessories should suit personality. Combs, hair clips, headbands, tiaras lend themselves to dainty floral adornment, but should be worn only if becoming to the individual.

Sharp scissors, pruners, and a wire cutter head the list of desirable equipment. Needle and thread are used to sew flowers on a hat or string them for a lei. A punch, made by grinding a tiny screwdriver to a point, is excellent to pierce pods and cones. If the man of the house has an electric drill, so much the better. Scotch tape, cotton, a pencil, candle, paraffin, and stapler are used on occasion. Once assembled, the corsage materials can be kept together in a box or basket ready for instant use. A fisherman's metal tackle box is ideal.

PLATE III

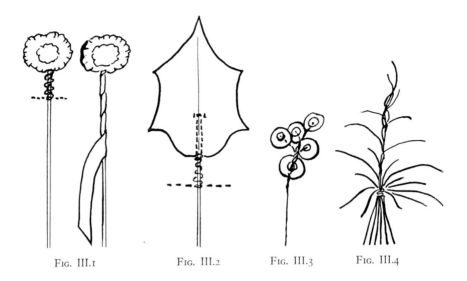

Fig. III.1   Fig. III.2   Fig. III.3   Fig. III.4

Material: Variegated ivy leaves, white clover blossoms, pittosporum
leaves from inner branches of the shrub.

Form: Square with accent point at top.

Line: Subtle Hogarth curve within the square.

Color harmony: Analogous—green and white.

Texture: Smooth, glossy leaves; smooth, dull ribbon; soft, prickly
clover.

Finishing: Green stem ends cut straight across to harmonize with
square form. White-edged green ribbon to repeat the analogous
harmony.

Technique:

Cut clover stem ½ inch below the head. Tape the short stem
to prevent cutting by the wire. Using 6-inch lengths of 32-gauge
wire, twist around tape close under clover head (Fig. III.1).
Wrap wire stems with green floral tape. Using 28-gauge wire, wire
the pittosporum leaf rosette the same way, beginning just under the
lowest leaf. Preliminary taping is not necessary.

Wire the ivy leaf by making a hairpin of a 14-inch wire. Insert the
ends on both sides of the midrib as shown in Fig. III.2 and pull down

PLATE III

Variegated Ivy, White Clover, and Pittosporum in a Pointed Square to the lower end of the leaf, wrapping one wire around the short petiole and the other wire. Straighten and cover with tape.

There are many small units in this corsage as each clover is wired separately. If all the stems are gathered at one point the corsage is too heavy. To lighten the construction, group the clovers at the top in a bunch, and consolidate the fine stems into one by twisting tightly around each other (Fig. III.3). Group the clovers at the lower right the same way. Place ivy, pittosporum, and clover stems in position and bind tightly at assembly point with 32-gauge wire. Assembly point is at apex of 3 ivy leaves. Bend lower material into position (Fig. III.4). Cut stem ends off on a straight line.

Make a full bow of green and white taffeta ribbon and tie securely around corsage at assembly point. Arrange loops so that they fill the lower left corner of square form.

Corsage by: Mrs. Samuel Dunlap.

IV

PREPARING THE FLOWERS

The beauty and durability of the corsage depends entirely on its underpinnings. The finished product should be light in weight, but securely put together.

The basic principle of corsage construction is the substitution of wire for the natural flower stems. There are several reasons for this. (1) Wire is lighter and less bulky than the natural stems. (2) It is flexible and can be maneuvered as desired. (3) It is rigid enough to hold the completed design in position. (4) Proper wiring will prevent flowers from shattering or falling out of the corsage.

Therefore, the corsage is made up of individual flowers with flexible wire stems. The assembled wire stems form the skeleton of the corsage.

Although there is no limit to the flowers and foliages that may be used in corsages, a few basic techniques can be adapted for use on almost any blossom or leaf that takes your fancy. It is well to begin with the simplest wiring methods and gradually master the more complicated techniques.

Green corsage wire is used in 9-, 12-, and 18-inch lengths. The 26- and 28-gauges are suitable for most flowers. Heavier 24-gauge is used for weighty flowers, and 18- to 22-gauge may be necessary for bouquets. Fine 32-gauge wire is used for delicate flowers like violets, and is also used to assemble the individually wired flowers into the design. To avoid bulkiness, always select the finest wire that is consistent with the weight of the blossom. If it is too fine, it will not be strong enough to hold the top-heavy flower in position. If the wire is too heavy, the corsage will be uncomfortable to wear.

Begin by cutting all stems to 1 inch. Condition flowers with a long drink of water as in the preceding chapter. Some flowers require special treatment. (See Chart I in Appendix.) After proper conditioning, the flowers are ready to be wired.

An 18-inch wire is chosen to allow a double stem. This makes it practical to use a light-weight wire, which causes less abuse to the flower than a single heavier wire. The long wire stems are necessary for assembling the design; any surplus can be cut off when this is completed. If the corsage is a petite design, use the shorter 12-inch length. Stemming by the *single-wire method* is best for heavier flowers where a heavier wire is used.

The simplest method, the one you will use for nearly three-fourths of the flowers, is *the clutch method,* illustrated in Fig. 9. Bend the 18-inch piece of wire just short of the center. Place the short side on a parallel with the natural flower stem with the bend in the wire as high as possible under the flower head. Hold stem and wire securely together. Then, beginning where you bent the wire, twist the longer half securely around the stem and the parallel wire several times until you come to the end of the natural flower stem. Then straighten the remainder of the wire you have been twisting and make it parallel with the other half. This gives the flower a new, double, flexible stem approximately 9 inches long. Daffodils, gerberas, and Dutch iris are representative of flowers taking this method of preparation.

Some flowers have very fragile stems that break off when an attempt is made to wrap wire around them, no matter how gently it is done. For protection, wrap the stem or tube with floral tape before wiring (see Fig. 10). Hold the end of the tape in place high under the flower. Wrap around stem tightly, stretching as you twist. Then wire as shown in Fig. 9. A wisp of cotton, moistened after it is placed, may be substituted for the tape. Examples are individual delphinium florets, cosmos, and eucharis lilies. For fragile trumpet flowers, place a ball of moist cotton in the curve of a hairpin wire and push it down deep inside the trumpet.

Flowers that snap from the stem easily, or have no stem at all, are treated as shown in Fig. 11. Take a 4-inch length of wire, called a guide wire. Cut the end on a slant to make it sharper. Push the guide wire up through the center of the stem into the very top of the blossom (Fig.

11a). If the stem is too fragile for the wire to go through it, put the guide wire parallel to the stem and then push into the blossom. Stop just short of the surface of the flower so the wire will not show from the top. Chrysanthemums and calendulas are wired like this. In some cases, as with doronicum and strawflower, it may be necessary to push the guide wire up through the top of the blossom, then bend the end into a little hook (Fig. 11c) and pull the wire back down from the bottom until it is out of sight on top. Then use the 18-inch length of wire and proceed as in Fig. 9 (see also Fig. 11b).

Roses have a strong calyx. Although they may be wired as in Fig. 11, a better method is the one used for carnations. Push the 18-inch length of wire horizontally through the green calyx until there is an equal amount of wire on each side to pull down vertically for the stem (Fig. 12). Twist one end around the other a few times. This is *the piercing method*. The 9-inch length of heavier wire works well for heavy flowers; some corsage-makers prefer it. The only difference in wiring is that the one wire end, which twists about the natural stem, stops short under the stem. In either technique, if the wire buckles when you try to force it into the calyx, select a heavier gauge.

FIG. 9   FIG. 10   FIG. 11   FIG. 12

Fragile little flowers like violets and pansies are grouped, stagger fashion, and bound together in little bunches with fine 32-gauge wire (Fig. 13). It may be necessary to tape the stems first, as in Fig. 10.

Wire tiny spray flowers (Poetaz narcissus, bridal wreath, and scilla) and branches of berries (pyracantha, holly, and jasmine) by hooking the wire up into the lower part of the cluster and twisting one end a few times around the stem. Then straighten ends to full length (Fig. 14).

Gardenias are very touchy and require special treatment, as shown in Figs. 15a and 15b. They will discolor at the least abuse. When handling, moisten the fingers. Cut off green calyx but leave white tube intact. Place a cardboard gardenia collarette under the blossom at once by turning the blossom upside down and pushing the collarette over the tube. This protects the petals and holds them out to their full circumference. Tape the tube under the collarette and wire as in Fig. 9. Gardenia buds have a rare twist and exquisite form. Tape and wire in the same manner, but do not use the collarette.

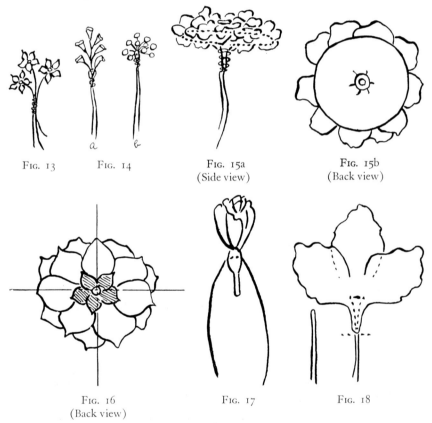

FIG. 13   FIG. 14   FIG. 15a   FIG. 15b
                                  (Side view)   (Back view)

FIG. 16   FIG. 17   FIG. 18
(Back view)

Special mention needs to be made for wiring camellias. They are favorites where they grow outdoors in the South and on the West Coast, and as hothouse flowers in colder climates. The blossoms are heavy, and some lose their heads easily. If the variety is secure on the stem, wire as Fig. 9. If it is insecure, use the method shown in Fig. 16. Push two wires at right angles entirely through the lower part of the blossom or the upper part of the calyx. Pull down gently, shape to fit under the underside of the flower, and straighten for the stem. You may find it necessary for some varieties to use the technique of the little guide wire pushed up through the center of the flower, bent into a hook and secured, as in Fig. 11. Use the finest wire possible for treating camellias, but if it buckles at being pushed into the flower, a heavier gauge is indicated.

Buds are used frequently in artistic corsage designs. Fig. 17 indicates the customary wiring method, which is to push the wire directly through the calyx as in Fig. 12. If the calyx is too small (freesia and fuchsia) and it is impractical to push the wire through the lower petals, merely tape the end of the bud as in Fig. 10 and then wire as in Fig. 9.

Fig. 18 shows the technique for preparing individual petals for corsage use. Form a hairpin loop of fine wire, push two ends through the base of the petal from the front side and carefully press the wires flat against the lower side of the blossom at the back and pull down the ends carefully to make the stem. A single sewing stitch with the wire may be used if you find it easier. This is the technique used in the Duchess form (like making the outer part of a large Glamellia). Assembling the parts is described in Chapter VI.

TAPING

Floral tape, a rubberized tape with various trade names, is used in the next step of corsage construction. Wire each flower that is to be used in the design. Then cover each wire with tape.

In some corsages, the tape is a conspicuous part of the design, but in most it serves a utilitarian purpose only. But it generally shows, even if just on the stem ends, and should harmonize with the color scheme. Floral tape is available in nearly all the pastel colors. Green and white are the favorites. Black is used for men's formal boutonnieres, and brown is smart for dried materials.

There is a definite art to putting the tape on securely. Take the wired flower in one hand. Hold the end of the tape over the highest point of the wire under the flower. Wrap tape securely around the wire by twirling the flower—by the stem, not by the blossom—pulling tape down and *stretching* as you pull, so it completely covers all the wire and fits snugly around it. Pinch off tape at wire ends.

FIG. 19a   FIG. 19b   FIG. 20

FIG. 21a   FIG. 21b   FIG. 21c. Sweetpea from
                                            two rose petals

Fig. 19 shows two taping examples. In (a), the tape begins at the top of the stem. In (b), a rose bud, the wire has been pushed through the calyx, and tape is put around the calyx to cover the wire and is carried down the stem. If tape doesn't hold on the first round, repeat. It sticks to itself.

When working with minute flowers or jewelry designs, cut the tape in half lengthwise to provide long, narrow strips.

Tape may be used for protective purposes. We mentioned taping fragile flowers before wiring them (Fig. 10). Tape is also used to make a calyx on buds where there is none. In wiring individual petals (Fig. 18) for the Duchess flower, it may be necessary to place a little strip of tape horizontally on the back of the petal before putting the wire through it (Fig. 20).

The feathered type of corsage is attractive and easy to make. Carnations and chrysanthemums are the favorites. The purpose of feathering is to give a light note where full blooms are too heavy and buds are not available. Separate the large blossom into sections. Gather the petals together in a group. Tape the group at the base, making the tape serve as a calyx, and you have created a small flower (Fig. 21a). Then wire as indicated and cover the wires (Fig. 21b). The technique is the same as that shown in Fig. 9.

This same technique is used to make a "sweet pea" from the outer petals of a full blown rose (Fig. 21c). Dip rose in cold water before removing petals. Fold two petals in the center lengthwise. Fit the outer one into the upright one and carefully bend down the tip of the outer petal. Wrap petals tightly together at the base with a small piece of tape. Wire as in Fig. 21b with fine wire.

Tape may be used as a decorative note by fashioning it into cord, as outlined in the chapter on "The Finishing Touch." And for an unusually gay corsage, wrap satin ribbon over the taped stems or use the satin surface adhesive-backed ribbon.

PLATE IV

The basic materials used in corsage craft are wire and tape. The wire shown upper right is 24 and 28 gauge. Other gauges that may be used are 26, 22, and 18. Very fine 32-gauge wire, known as hair wire, is used for assembling and for wiring fragile flowers. The lower the number of the gauge, the heavier and coarser the wire.

The floral tape being wrapped around a zinnia stem is stretchable, and covers the wires for protection. Floral tape comes in nearly all colors, with leaf green and light yellow-green being the most popular and white and orchid next in importance. The gloriosa leaves at center left have been wired and taped preparatory to being assembled into a design.

Chenille wire in many colors, pictured upper left, may be used as a stem as shown here with a gladiolus blossom. This eliminates taping. Chenille is also used for finishing touches, as described in Chapter VII. The gold and silver cords, with or without wire inserts, are used like chenille but are a little more elegant. Scrolls and a curlicue are shown in the center.

The rolls of ribbon shown upper right are the two-toned variety. Others that are popular are taffeta, satin, velvet, picot, and metallic. Paper and plastic colored colonial collars for nosegay corsages come in many sizes from the tiny ones used for place cards and wristlets to the largest ones chosen for wedding bouquets.

The succulent corsage at lower left shows the use of pine needles to lighten the effect of the heavy florets.

PLATE IV

Basic Materials of Wire and Tape

V

PREPARING THE FOLIAGE

Foliage can make or break the corsage. The days are gone when every corsage was backed with a limp, flat piece of asparagus fern. Now, foliage is not a filler, but a definite part of the design. It provides the accent or the finishing touch. Entire corsages made of foliage are new, different, and exotic. Foliage hats are fascinating.

As with flowers, the garden offers all sorts of leaves that may be used effectively in corsages, and many of them will provide new inspirations. Frequently you will prefer the leaf of the flower used, especially in the case of roses, carnations, camellias, and gardenias. Often, however, foliage that is unique in color, texture, or form builds up an otherwise mediocre design. Maple, oak, magnolia, croton, huckleberry, and gladiolus foliage are then chosen. Investigate the large family of conifers, for they open a new field of interest with their variety of forms and textures. Pine, yew, cedar, and juniper are favorites. The broad-leaved evergreens such as rhododendron, salal, Oregon grape, and ligustrum begin a list that may be combined with conifers for variety. Cyclamen and begonia leaves add still another textural quality, and crinkly geranium foliage is used for frilly effects. Most ferns are so fragile that they are not very suitable.

Smilax, ivy, and other dainty vines are adaptable to the diagonal or surplice type of floral decoration that sweeps from one shoulder to the opposite hip, or for trailing bouquets.

Corsage foliages are not restricted to green. Instead, the colored leaves are sought to finish a harmony, and the variegated leaves are used for effect. Yellow coleus, pink caladium, and silvery-blue carnation leaves are only a few of the colored foliages available. If you are really stumped for colored leaves for an analogous harmony, visit your vegetable patch or super market. The burnt-orange and creamy tones of rhubarb leaves are a challenge to the designer. Dubonnet and wine tinted beet foliage not only fills a color need but has delightful curves besides. A third favorite is mahogany kale, or the yellow variety that takes on chartreuse tints. For leaf accents or foliage flowers, these vegetables are distinctive.

The Foliage Accent

Foliage has several important functions in the corsage:

(1) To vary the texture when the smooth surface of leaves is needed to relieve fussy flowers.

(2) To supply contrast. In a wedding bouquet, a background of green leaves makes the white flowers show up against the white gown. Likewise, a corsage of pink roses on a pink dress is lost without a frame of dark foliage.

(3) To add color and weight at the focal point in the design.

(4) To provide the finishing touch of the corsage, with bows and loops of foliage instead of ribbon.

(5) To add the trailing element in bouquets.

Let the design speak for itself. If it does not need foliage for any of these purposes, do not put any in. However, if the corsage seems incomplete, experiment with foliage to heighten the effect. But keep the line and form of the corsage in mind, and make the foliage an integral part of the entire design.

Conditioning

Like flowers, foliage must be conditioned and tested for durability. See instructions in Chapter III, and special notations in the chart at the end of the book.

If a leaf of a certain color and texture is appropriate, but is too large for the design, cut it down to the desired size. Either use the natural top and trim the bottom, or vice versa. Caladium, loquat, viburnum, and oak leaves may be trimmed to fit the need. Notice that this technique is used on the croton leaves shown in Plate V. Beautiful reddish-purple "leaves" are made from petals of the banana blossom.

Wiring Foliage

The simplest leaf wiring and the technique used for three-fourths of the favorite foliages, is *the clutch method,* shown in Fig. 22. Simply twist one end of the wire around the petiole directly under the blade at the same time wrapping it around the other half of the wire and the short natural stem. Bring wire ends down vertically to form a flexible stem. Ligustrum, photinia glabra, and dogwood are examples for this type of wiring.

FIG. 22   FIG. 23   FIG. 24   FIG. 25   FIG. 26

Fig. 23 shows the technique for a leaf that is of poor substance, or one that is apt to come loose from the stem. Bend the wire into a hairpin in the middle. Thrust the ends through the front of the leaf with one end on each side of the midrib just above the base. Flatten out the two ends carefully on the back of the leaf and bring down for the stem, twisting one around the other. If you wish a decided curve in the leaf, pierce the midrib about halfway up. Peony and hydrangea foliage take this technique.

Leaves with leaflets, like rose and box, are wired by hooking the hairpin wire just above the lowest pair of leaves, and twisting a few times around the stem (Fig. 24).

Little tufts of carnation foliage lend variety in form as well as delightful color. Group the little tufts together to make the size desired. Twist wire tightly around the short stems two or three times to hold securely. Use this method for groups of little narrow leaves of crocus, cornflower, or broom (Fig. 25).

Strap-like leaves are excellent accents in the design. Iris, daffodil, and tulip leaves can be used in several ways. Fig. 26a shows a single leaf end, or a portion of a leaf cut on a slant at the desired length. Gather at the base as if you were sewing, wrap the wire a few times around the gathered base, and straighten wire ends. A loop of foliage (Fig. 26b) is made by doubling a 6- or 8-inch leaf, gathering the two ends together, and wiring as above. A wide tulip leaf is managed by gathering it at the base and wiring as above (Fig. 26c). If the ends slip out of the twisted wires, pierce wire through ends of leaf and then wrap around the base. Wire-like foliage of white rain lilies (zephyranthes) is effective if looped in varying lengths as shown in Fig. 26d.

Foliage bows are easily made of these and other long, narrow leaves. Make into loops as Fig 26b, wiring through center of double length, or assemble several leaves wired as Fig. 26a or 26b in one place in the corsage.

When the design calls for a round circle of leaves, as in the holly corsage illustrated in Plate XI, use a gardenia collarette as a base, staple the leaves to it in the desired position, and pull stem of center flower through the middle. This same treatment may be used for a tailored corsage of a single peony, gardenia, camellia, or tuberous begonia, although generally the leaves are wired and arranged individually. Some camellias have the leaves so artistically placed under the flower, with the right side up, that they may be left undisturbed on the stem.

Since most evening corsages call for brilliant finishing touches, foliage is generally restricted to daytime designs unless it is glamourized as are the silvered ivy leaves in Plate I.

Foliage is taped with the same stretching procedure used for flowers. Be sure that all wires are covered if possible with the exception of the wires on the top side of the leaf when the hairpin technique shown in Fig. 23 is used. Only a tiny portion of the wire will show if it is properly done, and its color makes it inconspicuous.

THE FOLIAGE FLOWER

Some of the most original and spectacular corsages are made entirely of foliage. Try a grouping of coleus leaves in various sizes and form them into a crinkly devastating Joseph's coat flower. Caladium leaves will make a fetching corsage if the individual leaves are looped (Fig. 26b) and put together in a rounded rose form. Variegated ivy with its creamy border, green center, and pointed ends is easily fashioned into a modern tailored flower. A croton corsage is in high favor whether from florist shop or southern garden.

Try the possibilities of leaves that are growing in your garden. Begonia, red amaranthus, variegated Chinese evergreen, wandering jew, pelargonium, skimmia, and rhododendron are only a few of the materials available. Predominantly foliage designs are colorful. One daylily blossom surrounded by mottled croton leaves is as bright as a summer's day. Red photinia glabra leaves harmonize with red miniature dahlias.

THE SUCCULENTS

The succulent family offers wonderful shapes from little nubby round forms to large flat leaves. The subtle colors range from gray to soft blush and open a whole new field of experimentation. The frosty-looking surfaces of most of the succulents are refreshing on a hot day and give your costume a crisp, cool appearance.

Succulent corsages will last for several weeks if kept in a cool place between wearings. Furthermore, the leaves may be rooted after the corsage is dismantled.

An exotic arrangement may be made of three clusters of the common "hen and chickens." A sturdy guide wire pushed well up into the head of the flower (Fig. 11) holds it securely. Care must be taken that the succulent corsage is not too heavy for comfortable wear. Notice the attractive succulent corsage on the workshop table in Plate IV.

PLATE V

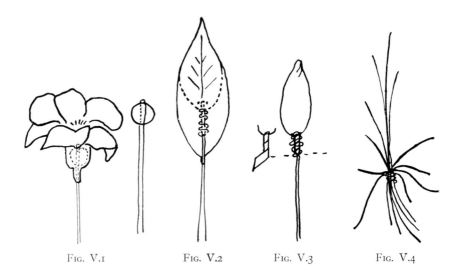

Fig. V.1   Fig. V.2   Fig. V.3   Fig. V.4

Material: Allamanda blossoms, croton leaves.

Form: Triangle.

Line: Diagonal.

Color harmony: Analogous. Yellow, yellow-green, green.

Texture: Fragile, tissue paper blossoms, glossy, smooth leaves.

Finishing: Green stems.

Technique:

The exquisite allamanda blossom is fleeting and hence a special provision is made for its extended life. Take a ball of cotton a little smaller than the trumpet, moisten it, and place within the curve of a hairpin made of a 6-inch length of 28-gauge wire. Pull this wire down through the blossom, allowing the cotton to rest in the trumpet. This serves the additional purpose of holding the trumpet firm, making it a more desirable corsage flower (Fig. V.1). Wire the 5 open blossoms this way.

If the prettiest markings and colors are found on large croton leaves, cut leaf down as shown by the dotted line in Fig. V.2. Wire by putting a hairpin wire through the base of the leaf.

Wire the 4 buds and the partly opened flower shown at top on short stems of 9-inch 28-gauge wire (Fig. V.3), and assemble by taping

PLATE V

Triangle of Allamanda Blossoms with Croton Leaves

one on to another so only one stem remains. This technique reduces unnecessary weight. Add the 5 open blossoms and the 5 leaves, making the assembly point under the center flower (Fig. V.4). Turn the remaining leaves back on their wires. Cut stems to square out the triangle. No ribbon is needed, as the decorative leaves are sufficient.

Corsage by: Glad Reusch.

VI

ASSEMBLING

The flowers and leaves you are going to use have been wired and taped individually. Now they are ready to be assembled into the design. The design is the pleasing pattern achieved by placement of the solids and voids.

In the chapter on "Design" we discussed the various points that make up the design: form, line, color, texture, proportion, and balance. Put the individual parts of the corsage together, keeping these factors in mind as you work.

The dominant flowers should face the front. There should be a feeling of third dimension which is achieved by putting some of the important flowers higher or lower, so all will not be on one plane. Keep the flowers far enough apart to get the most expansive effect from the design, but do not allow too much of the skeleton to show. Where the form of the individual flowers is of utmost importance, see that each bloom has its own sphere of influence. The flowers should never be crowded.

Do not let the appearance of the corsage be topheavy. There should be one focal point, so the eye goes through the composition easily and comes to rest there. A strong focal point can be attained by a large bloom, deep color, or special textural value. The light notes of the corsage should be about the edges.

In most designs there is one assembly point in the construction. It is placed at the focal point, which gives the weight of the corsage there and makes for better balance. The individual wire stems are fastened together at the assembly point, and the design radiates from this point.

Each plate in the book is accompanied by sketches showing the construction of the various corsages. The skeleton sketches indicate the assembly point of each one, showing you the technique for assembling the various types of designs.

The Spray Corsage

The simplest spray type of corsage is made with five blooms, let us say daffodils. The construction is illustrated in Fig. 27 and the procedure is as follows. First wire and tape each of the five flowers. Select the smallest flower for the top of the corsage and hold it in your left hand. Add a second bloom slightly to the left below the first. Then add the third stagger-fashion to the right. Bind the three together very tightly about 1 inch below the third blossom. If corsage is heavy, use fine 32-gauge wire and wrap it around and around the three stems in one place. If design is light in weight, bind with tape by circling tightly several times. This establishes the assembly point. Then place the fourth blossom with the stem parallel to the other three stems, but bend it so the flower is slightly downward. Bind at assembly point. Then place the fifth blossom, bend the stem, and bind at same place. Cover assembly wire with tape.

The daffodil corsage may be further embellished by loops of daffodil foliage. Make according to directions in Chapter V and place among the flowers, fastening wire stems securely at assembly point.

An entirely different effect is produced if buds are used in the composition. Lacking buds, remove the outer sepals or perianth and use the trumpet alone for a smaller form.

This same group of five daffodils may be assembled into a tapering end corsage by the use of tiny spring bulbous flowers, pussy willows, or other small blooms as outlined for the corsage in Figs. 28 and 29. The daffodils may also be assembled in a line, crescent, or chain technique. These same instructions apply to any other dominant flowers.

The Two-way Corsage

This type corsage is usually made of small flowers, either tubular such as stephanotis, hyacinth bells, or round stock florets. The flowers are all prepared with wire and tape and then assembled one by one. Starting at each end with one blossom and holding the stems at the center, additional flowers are added, alternately, from the top and bottom at the same time. The shape builds out from the point to a broadened triangle toward the center on each side. The bow is placed at the center and the wired blossoms arranged symmetrically on each side. Where there is a shortage of flowers small tufts of ribbon (one small loop and a slanted end) may be wired and taped and placed among the blossoms just as if they were flowers. Cut off wire stems at back near center. (Plate XX shows a two-way corsage.)

Assembling with Tape

Where many small flowers are used in a design, as the snapdragons in Fig. 29, the individual flowers are wired on short stems about 5 inches long to avoid a heavy accumulation of wires. These short stems may be attached together stagger-fashion with tape instead of binding

Fig. 27   Fig. 28   Fig. 29

at one assembly point with wire. Fig. 28 illustrates the technique, which is ideal for azaleas, tiny roses, volets, and small flower buds. This type of assembling is used for spaced designs such as those required in the wristlet and hair-do. It may also be used for heavier flowers like gladioli in a trailing design such as the bouquet shown in Plate XIII.

THE TAPERING-END CORSAGE

Where no stems show, the corsage is constructed so the composition will come to a point at each end, or at the trailing end in a jabot design that has the wide part of the triangle at the top.

Fig. 29 illustrates a corsage made of snapdragons and petunias in a Hogarth curve line with tapering ends. Wire the snaps individually as in Fig. 12, and the petunias as in Fig. 10. Assemble the snaps with tape as described for Fig. 28. Then assemble the corsage the same as Fig. 27 (the daffodils) turning the lower sprays of snapdragons back on themselves. Cut all stems off short at the focal point, which is just under the largest petunia at the center of the design.

THE CHAIN TECHNIQUE AND THE LEI

There are two methods of assembling flowers in the chain technique. Tuberoses, stephanotis, and hyacinths are dropped into one another by being pushed on to a wire (Fig. 30). Necklace chains, short pointed sprays to use with dominant flowers, wristlets, hair-dos, flower bows, and initials are created in this manner. Flat flowers may be strung close together in the same way on wire or thread (Fig. 31).

When the design calls for a flat row of flowers facing out, as for a dog collar or flower belt, remove the stems and string on a wire through the calyx of each blossom (Fig. 32). If the flowers are heavy, it is better to wire separately with fine 32-gauge wire, tape, and assemble with tape.

A marvelous feeling of warmth, hospitality, and friendship accompanies the presentation of a lei. In the Hawaiian Islands, fragrance is important. Frangipani, ginger, pikake, and vanda orchid (Miss Joachim) are desirable lei flowers, although nearly every round flower that is a good keeper is used. Among flowers suitable for leis on the mainland or in the Islands are carnation, gardenia, marigold, aster, pansy, lantana, cornflower, delphinium (florets), azalea, rhododendron, calendula, chrysanthemum, clivia, miniature zinnia, gaillardia, hollyhock, marguerite, double petunia, scabiosa, turk's cap and straw-flower.

A lei is made by either of the chain techniques, depending on type of flowers, except that stringing is done with nylon or No. 8 cotton thread and an 8-inch needle. The lei is generally 36 to 40 inches long. If two or three leis are to be worn at once, use flowers of different size, form, and color, and graduate the lengths.

THE COLONIAL DESIGN

The colonial corsage is a circular form that has been prominent in floral art through the ages. It is largely used for bouquets, and the complex construction is found in Chapter X. However, small-sized corsages made in the colonial manner are charming, especially for the teen-age girl. A petite design of miniature flowers arranged in the colonial is effective floating in party fingerbowls.

A delightful colonial corsage may be made with a pink rose in the center surrounded by purple violets interspersed with tiny white alyssum and finished with a miniature lace collar.

Wire the center flower with a long wire. Wire the violets and alyssum in groups of three as shown in Fig. 13, using wire only long enough to bind at the assembly point which is the stem of the center rose. The first row is on shorter stems than the outer row. It is not necessary to tape each stem in colonial construction, as the blossoms fit so closely together that the stems do not show from the top. Add three or four groups of small flowers, bind tightly to the center wire, and continue to add until the center flower is completely surrounded. If another row of flowers is desired, use slightly longer stems and add around the outside in the same way. It is important that the center flower be raised slightly above the outer rows.

Cut off the bulky wires on a slant. Turn the corsage upside down and slip the collar over the stems. Net, lacelon, leaves (real or artificial), or ribbon may circle the flowers instead of a plastic or paper collarette. Bind stems all at once with floral tape. Add ribbon loops and streamers if desired. For large colonial, bend stems to form a handle. The taped handle may be covered with satin ribbon for more elegance.

Fig. 30   Fig. 31   Fig. 32

Dual Flowers

Many buds or small blossoms may be inserted into another flower or floret to make a new effect. Examples are a rosebud or gladiolus bud in a gladiolus flower; a rosebud or small orchid in a spider chrysanthemum, or an azalea bud in an azalea blossom. Interesting color combinations may be achieved by using different color values.

Fig. 33 indicates the assembling technique of a rosebud in a gladiolus flower. Wire the bud securely as in Fig. 17. Open up the gladiolus flower, remove the stamen and pistil, and insert the bud in the center, closing the petals around it. Secure the two together by pushing a wire completely through the lower section horizontally and tape. Fig. 34 shows a corsage made of five such flowers.

Marigolds or trollius may be used with daylilies, and gardenias with Easter lilies. The contrast of the dark center of a calendula in a daylily is good, and the calendula makes the daylily stay open longer. See Plate II.

The Duchess Flower

Inserting a smaller bud into a petaled form is the basic construction of the duchess flower. Plate VI shows a Glamellia, the duchess form made of gladioli. One bud, several half-open flowers, and some fully open blossoms are used progressively for this effect.

If desired, use individual petals of flowers and wire as in Fig. 18. Then assemble around the center flower or group of flowers. Reverse pink tulip petals and place them around violets, or surround ranunculus with talisman rose petals.

Other combinations of flowers and petals for duchess flowers include rose forms made of geranium leaves, poinsettia petals centered with pyracantha or holly berries, pink anemones surrounded by rubrum lily petals, epidendrum orchid clusters (or other small cluster flowers) in the midst of several rows of red daylily petals, and pink garden dianthus with the exotic petals of the gloriosa lily, just as they mature a rich ruby red. Check color combinations carefully in this type of design.

FIG. 33   FIG. 34   FIG. 35

THE EPAULET

The epaulet, worn over the edge of the shoulder and down over the arm, is built up in three sections as shown in Fig. 35. The two outer lengths are even, the center one longer. Assemble the sprays with tape, making them wider as they reach the assembly point. Join the three groups and bend to fit the arm, then add required flowers at the center. Try it on as you work. Pinks, roses, asters, ranunculus, and sweet peas are attractive for the epaulet, though if you are ambitious you can make a beautiful design of tiny clustered ixora.

There is no recipe for assembling a good corsage. Imagination, originality, and a flair for something different will result in artistic creations. Don't be afraid to try unusual combinations, thinking in terms of good line first and color second. And always key your designs to the fashions of the day.

PLATE VI

FIG. VI.1 FIG. VI.2 FIG. VI.3 FIG. VI.4 FIG. VI.5 FIG. VI.6

Material: Gladiolus and fern.

Form: Circle/triangular.

Line: Concentric petals in the "Glamellia" and cut buds to show horizontal note, giving periphery a unique variation with fern lace work.

Color Harmony: Apricot and green.

Texture: Smooth undressed kid, glossy foliage, shiny ribbon.

Finishing: Show sufficient weight in stems to balance, and deep apricot satin bow and ends to fill in the triangle. A green ribbon would be equally fitting.

Technique:

Wire the two buds by piercing through the base, 26-gauge medium wire, twist around stem, tape (Fig. VI.1). Treat half-open buds in same manner. Green calyx is left on buds.

Wire the piece of fern by piercing a hairpin wire, vertically, near the base. Tape (Fig. VI.3).

Symmetry for the Glamellia is accomplished by first wiring the central bud (Fig. VI.2), cut horizontally to expose a beautiful colored throat.

Pierce lower base with two crisscross wires, 26-gauge, to stabilize the flower bud. Pull down the wires and use one to twist about the other wires to form stem. Open a glad gently, remove stamen, and nestle the bud into the open corolla. Fold corolla about bud. Wire through bud and corolla, twist about base, clutch method (Fig. VI.4).

PLATE VI

Gladiolus, Forming a "Glamellia," with Fern

Separate a number of glads into petals. Choose the large, best textured petals. Place two or three together, one on top of the other. Pierce each group through near base, twist wire gently about base to form stem, and tape with narrow width. (Cut tape in half lengthwise and tape around stem for about ½ inch.) (Fig. VI.5). Prepare seven or eight groups with fine 30-gauge wire. Place one group after the other around the central flower until you have achieved a fine circle.

Assemble by starting with the two buds and upper cut bud at top and tape to hold position. Tape the second cut bud about the focal point. Attach the glamellia at the same spot and add fern by curving back on itself and attaching to the rest of corsage at the focal point (Fig. VI.6).

Cut off some of the wires short to reduce the weight. Arrange remaining wires carefully under the flower to present a balanced corsage. Pull tape down over cut ends of stems. Attach bow. Instead of the fern, the narrow leaves of the glad may be looped and used as a bow.

Corsage by: Glad Reusch.

VII

THE FINISHING TOUCH

Often the distinctive note of a corsage is achieved by the finishing touch. This may be made by the twist or turn of the taped stems, the fine line added by the gold and silver cord, or the textural quality of chenille wire or ribbon bows.

The finishing is an integral part of the design and should add to the beauty of the flowers but not overpower them. Don't use additional material unless the design needs it, but don't underestimate the value of the finishing touch.

A certain number of wired stem ends remain after the corsage is assembled. What to do with these ends is an important matter. The wires may be cut so no ends are exposed, or some of the stems may be cut short under the flowers and only a few dominant ends allowed to remain. Or, the wires may be arranged in a line of motion so they will continue the line of the design.

Fig. 36 indicates some favorite movements for stem endings. The line of a triangular daytime corsage is accented by the straight wide base of wires as in (a). Balance is added by irregularly cut wires as in (b). The curved line (c) is always a pleasing movement as it follows the neckline curve. This same group of curves is used to complete the "S" or Hogarth curve when the flowers are curved in the opposite direction.

The simple scroll with a single curve is an easy and effective finishing touch. The scrolls may all be on one side of the corsage (Fig. 37a) or divided in direction (Fig. 37b) depending on the line of design. To make the scrolls, hold the wire stem flat with the left hand. Using the tip end as the center of the coil, twist up the stem with the right hand until the coil reaches the desired size. The scrolls may be placed as shown, or arranged singly among the flowers as background.

The pencil twist, sketched in Fig. 37c, is made by holding the wire near the top of the pencil with the left hand and twisting it tightly about the pencil with the right hand until the desired number of twirls is made. Slide the pencil out, and the equally placed curls remain. This is an effective stem ending. The twirls may be made of chenille wires and interspersed between the flowers. Use discretion, however, as overdoing this technique will detract from the blossoms.

Surplus wire cut off →

Wire turned back →

a   b   c   a   b   c   d

Fig. 36   Fig. 37

If more color is needed, these wire ends may be covered with ribbon before being shaped. Start ribbon about 1 inch below flower, wind around stem to top, reverse, and wrap to end. Tie end in knot at bottom of stem, and allow a short piece of ribbon to remain (Fig. 37d). Or, begin 1 inch from bottom, go to end, reverse, and wrap to top. Fasten ribbon out of sight under flower with Scotch tape or fine wire.

RIBBON, METALLIC WIRE, CHENILLE

A corsage is worn to show the beauty of the flowers. If the design is complete, omit the ribbon. The ribbon should definitely be subordinate to the floral part of the corsage. Sometimes, however, the ribbon enhances the design or serves as a link between the corsage and the costume.

Consider the occasion when deciding upon the ribbon. Most tailored corsages for daytime wear are smarter without ribbon, while the evening designs may go all the way to stardom.

There is suitable ribbon for each flower. Consider not only the color, but the width and the texture. Satin is pleasing with roses, taffeta with tulips, velvet with lilies and tuberous begonias. Silver and gold ribbons reflect lights at night.

Ribbon ½ inch wide is the usual corsage choice, but a narrower ribbon is more suitable for tiny flowers. By the same token, save your wide ribbons for bouquets or use it to "back" a corsage. To do this, cut a wide piece on a slant, pinch it at the center, attach by wire to completed design, and cover wire with tape. If ribbon is not stiff, tape alone will hold it. Stretch around ribbon and corsage frame. If a bow is used on the corsage, make it of the same color and texture as the backing ribbon, but in a narrower width.

The actual technique of making the bow is mastered easily if directions are followed step by step.

(1) Hold ribbon in left hand, allowing about 3 inches to hang for the end.

(2) Form a loop over the first finger and shirr across the width of the ribbon where you hold it in your left hand, giving it a gathered effect at that point.

(3) Make another loop at lower end and shirr at the center point. Repeat back and forth until you have the required number of loops (Fig. 38a).

(4) The bow may be held together through the center with wire or ribbon, the ends of which are used for attaching to the corsage. Ribbon is easier to slip off and on when the corsage is placed in the refrigerator between wearings. Use an 8-inch length of ribbon. Twist it several times through the center and then tie it around the shirred section of the bow (Fig. 38b). This takes practice, but keep working at it until the procedure comes with ease and the loops fall back into the left hand while tightening at the center, so the bow will not be flat.

(5) Place bow in position; tie securely to corsage skeleton with ends of 8-inch piece you used around center. Don't try to tie this piece around loops and corsage at once. Complete bow; then fasten to corsage.

(6) Trim ribbons on a slant to prevent raveling. Knots may be tied near ends of satin ribbon; metallic ribbons may be curled by pulling tightly across dull knife.

If you can make a bow, fluffy and not flat, continue technique you know. Loops may be of one size or vary in length. Two kinds or two colors of ribbon may be tied together for a strong accent note. Use less of one than the other. Scraps of wide 4- or 5-inch satin ribbon, cut on the diagonal, may be added to narrow loops for variety. Consider ribbons with picot edges for use with plain flowers. A bow of two different ribbons, as satin and silver or gold, laid one on top of the other and tied as if they were a single ribbon, adds color or texture. Or use narrow No. 2 ribbon placed on top of a wider No. 3 ribbon. Or try a braided bow. Select three lengths of ribbon, knot near top, and pin to a curtain. Plait to length desired, finish lower end with a knot, cut surplus on slant, tie into a bow. Depending on the design, little flowers may be tied or sewed on the streamers. If the ribbon surface seems too broad, tie a knot into the end of the loop or near the ends. Bows may be tied into the corsage at more than one point if they are needed to carry the color of the ribbon through the design for unity. Instead of bows, soft loops may be tied among the flowers. Arrange a loop and end of ribbon or a couple of loops, wire together, tape, and insert in corsage as if it were a flower.

Metallic wire cords and chenille serve a similar purpose and are chosen depending on the occasion and suitability. Loops, bows, leaf forms, football initials, sorority letters, and chatelaine chains are made of these materials. They may also be the basic forms for wristlets, necklaces, and hair bands.

The chatelaine corsage is made of two circular designs, one larger than the other, connected together and worn in close proximity. An attractive chatelaine is made of anemones and stock in lavender with yellow jasmine, connected with gold cords.

Where only a few exotic flowers are available, the corsage may be on a background of metallic or chenille wire. Small and large loops with trailing ends shown in Fig. 39a are one type of background. Another, Fig. 39b, is a circular platform with a vertical strip in the center on which to attach a single orchid or hibiscus so the petals will be raised from the dress.

FIG. 38   FIG. 39

FIG. 40

TAPE FOR FINISHING

The tape with which you wrapped the stems may be used for finishing also. Decorative forms may be made by twisting the tape and fashioning it into a loop (Fig. 40a), a heart (b), a leaf (c), or chatelaine chain (d). These same designs may be made of the metallic cords or chenille wire. Use red tape or chenille in the heart shape for a Valentine corsage, or yellow loops to back a yellow marguerite "daisy won't tell" corsage.

Net, Maline, Lace

The colonial is usually surrounded with a lace, net, or maline ruffle. A baton design requires a ruffled edge also. A corsage for evening may be backed with a strip of wide net, lace, or milliner's horsehair braid.

Individual flowers such as roses and carnations may be circled with net ruffles before being assembled into the corsage. Little squares of net, pinched at the center, wrapped with wire and taped, may be worked into the design between the flowers.

Net bows and streamers are often used for large bouquets, while tiny wristlets may be fastened to a full net circle that is attached to an elastic band. Net muffs can be made up in advance, and a corsage added at the last minute.

Nylon net and veiling are desirable for corsage use, as dampness does not wilt them.

Foliage for Finishing

Natural foliage is an excellent finishing touch and was treated in a preceding chapter. However, artificial leaves may be made of voile, net, lace, velvet, or ribbon for special designs.

FIG. 41

Make a leaf frame of wire, as shown in Fig. 41, of a size and shape suitable to the design. Wind the frame with tape the same color as the covering you are going to use. Lay the tape-covered frame down on white paper, brush with fast-drying floral cement and cover with a piece of voile, net, lace, velvet, or ribbon. Turn over, brush cement on other side, and cover. Pull covering tight over frame, and cut surplus from edges with scissors. Orange-red voile leaves with gerberas make an eye-catching corsage.

The finishing materials and techniques shown in the plates throughout the book will give you ideas for similar finishing touches to adapt to your designs.

PLATE VII

FIG. VII.1   FIG. VII.2

Material: White chrysanthemums.
Form: Crescent.
Line: Semicircular.
Color harmony: White and chartreuse.
Texture: Fussy flowers alleviated by smooth ribbon.
Finishing: Ribbon bow with long streamers to dramatize the design.
Technique:

Cut the stems of the chrysanthemums ½ inch below the flower head. Cover the fragile short stems with floral tape. Using a 5-inch length of 28-gauge wire, twist one end around the stem and let the remaining long end serve as a stem. Cover with floral tape (Fig. VII.1).

Design the crescent by arranging the flowers on the table according to size. Starting with a bud, attach each flower to the one above it with a little piece of floral tape instead of binding wire. The secret is to keep the hair ornament light in weight. Stop when you reach the center flower (Fig. VII.2). Start with a bud at the top of the other side and make a curve that balances the first half. Join the two halves with tape. Make a bow and tie to the wire under the center flower.

While planned for a dramatic hair crescent for the very young, this arrangement will be equally at home about a chignon or braid if the streamers are omitted. Made smaller, it is chic as a pocket accessory.
Corsage by: Mrs. Arthur F. Coe.

62

PLATE VII

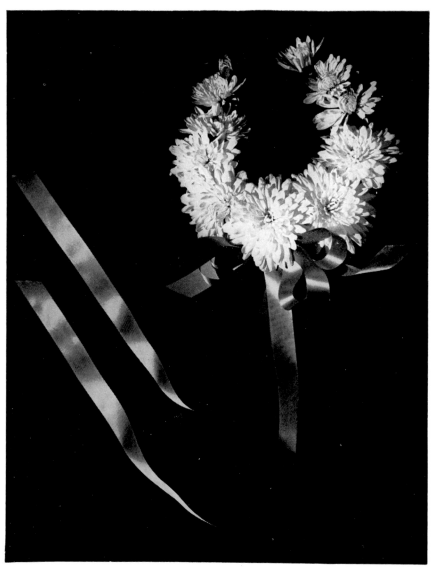

Crescent of White Chrysanthemums

VIII

OFF THE SHOULDER

The word "corsage" generally makes you think of a design to be worn on the shoulder. But this placement has been a little overdone through long years of use. Actually, the dictionary says a corsage is "a bouquet to be worn, originally at the waist." You will find it fun to wear your flowers off the shoulder and on the hair, neck, wrist, or ears; with your hat, bustle, pocket, and waistline offering other possibilities. If you plan your flower ornament with care, you can achieve a stunning effect.

Hair Ornaments and Hats

Let your current coiffure determine the design of your flowers for your hair. Each season's hair style calls for a different corsage line, just as it requires a new hat. Use a narrow spray to follow the diagonal part of your hair. A single blossom, known as the "tuck-in" moves around according to fashion. Two cerise roses in the hair with a matching velvet band at the throat will add distinction to an old frock. A crescent or complete circle of cornflowers fits snugly around the crown or chignon. Flowers tucked back of a braid are tantalizing if a bit of color shows from the front. Net tied around the head with a flower under the chin or at the shoulder fastening is a fascinating creation. The addition of a black velvet ribbon to the coiffure corsage is effective for a blonde. Companion spray pieces for a spectacular evening are worn one in the hair or the right side of the head, the other on the left shoulder. Bend slightly so the combined effect is a subtle Hogarth curve.

Fresh flowers are easily substituted for artificial hat trims, and are infinitely more charming. There's nothing better to give new life to your last year's bonnet. Use net or ribbon if it is needed for finishing or to tie in the color scheme. Border a cloche with zinnias and decorative wheat sprays. Or circle the crown of a sailor hat with cornflowers, poppies, and daisies. Make a cornucopia by rolling up a calla or galax leaf and fill it with tiny flowers such as valley lilies, daphne, or bouvardia for a peek-a-boo effect. Try single or double peonies flat on the brim of a picture hat. Grapes with chrysanthemums are a happy combination for late fall, and seasonal berries in bright colors accent a basic winter hat.

A designer's original is no more beautiful than the flower hats you can make for yourself. A hibiscus hat of eight blossoms with three pairs across the front and a single one at each end rests easily if attached to a wide circle made to your head size (Fig. 42). A second half-circle of wire placed at the back will help its stability.

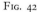

FIG. 42   FIG. 43

For evening, a skull cap of tiny flowers (hyacinths or stephanotis) wired in the chain technique and then interlaced as in Fig. 43 is a dream piece. For daytime, accent a plaited skull cap of daylily foliage with daylily blossoms. Keep the frame in the refrigerator and add fresh flowers daily.

Model your hat on your head as you work, using either a little beany or an acutal buckram assist. Experiment with paper pie plates for a crown and brim. Completely cover them with gardenia foliage by sewing the leaves on both sides of brim and open crown. Attach gardenia blossoms around the brim. For a cocktail hat, cover a little frame with wandering jew and highlight with parrot tulips. Or make a turban effect of small and large marigolds in shades of yellow and bronze. For a picture hat, cover a wire frame with net and scatter small flowers such as violas, stock florets, sweet peas, or bachelor buttons between the layers of net that make the brim.

Extremely modern hats may be made from tropical leaves from southern gardens or indoor houseplants. Caladium, spathyphyllum, coleus, sea grape, and stripped palm leaves are adaptable. The cut-out leaves of monstera give an unusual effect. The smart floral milliner may even use tree bark. The bark of madrona, the cloth-like fiber of palm, the punk tree, or melaleuca, and birch may be sewed or thonged for a tailored effect. Accent with a quill of yucca, pine needles, or Scotch broom.

FLORAL JEWELRY

Necklaces of flowers take the form of a choker, high neckline, Victorian necklace, bib, jabot, plunging V, surplice, or lei.

When velvet goes with the costume, use a single wide band of it around your neck. Fasten at the front with a single blossom or a tiny circle of little flowers wired in a chain. A colored band of chartreuse grosgrain, crossed at the front and fastened with a bunch of violets (Fig. 44) announces the arrival of spring. A dog collar may be made of medium-sized spoon or Korean chrysanthemums by stringing them lei-style on a wire. Put them only close enough together so the wire doesn't show, and allow enough wire at the ends for delicate taped loops to fasten. A double row is preferable for a long, slender neck or if the flowers are very small. If you want only an accent at the neckline, use three medium-sized blossoms at the center of a wire and tape the remainder of the wire with matching colored tape. If gold accessories are used, cover tape with gold ribbon.

In necklace designs, if flat composite flowers such as aster, didiscus, and geum are used, it is better to wire them separately with 32-gauge wire, tape, and assemble on a wire length with tape as described in Chapter VI and Fig. 28. This is the best method if a bib effect is desired at the center of the necklace as in Fig. 45.

A flower chain of hyacinths or lilies of the valley may have a medallion corsage at the end, silhouetted against ribbon loops and pinned to the top of a strapless dress. Plate VIII shows the combination of pearls and flowers that will give you ideas for other designs.

A jabot may be made of clustered flowers such as primrose or clivia and fitted to the neck opening of a suit. Or use narcissus and madroña and make earrings to match.

Bracelets are very simple. A flower chain constructed like a lei is

FIG. 44   FIG. 45   FIG. 46a

the easiest to make. Plastic forms especially for floral bracelets are available. For a home-made version, cover a piece of oval cardboard with satin and fasten to a covered elastic band. Pin the corsage to the oval. Or make a frame of looped metallic cords. A garland bracelet, wrapping the arm from glove to elbow may be made by assembling flowers closely with tape. Sweet peas in graduated colors, gerberas or pyrethrums are attractive for this design.

A flower solitaire ring is made by gluing a single blossom to an inexpensive frame.

EARRINGS

Choose for your earring design a form you like in jewelry. Flower earrings are made by gluing single or multiple blossoms to inexpensive frames. Plastic forms, from dime stores, shell or hobby shops have a smooth plastic base. If you choose metal frames, paint with clear nail polish to prevent tarnishing.

A quick-drying glue will secure flower to base. Remove stem completely and put glue on back of flower and on earring frame. Hold flower in place until glue adheres (Fig. 46a). Or you can wire the single blossom by pushing extra fine wire through the calyx and attaching flower to frame with the wire ends.

Any small, round flower is suitable for simple earrings made this way, but a fragrant flower, Grand Duke jasmine or fleur d'amour, is especially nice. When you wear a lei, use matching single flowers for earrings. The round design can be varied by using a bit of delicate foliage with a single flower, perhaps a Cecil Brunner rose with three leaflets (Fig. 46b). Wire flower and foliage together with very fine wire and either paste or wire to the frame.

A little plastic flower vase with earring attachment is simple to use for any single flower that is large enough to hide the vase. Put cotton around flower stem, wire and tape stem, and insert in container. Water in the vase will keep the flower fresh; cotton and wire will hold it securely (Fig. 46c).

The crescent (Fig. 46d) fits snugly into the curve of the ear lobe. If earring frames are unavailable in a shape you want, cut them out of light-weight cardboard and glue to circular base of frame. Delphinium florets are chosen for this crescent. Buds and/or foliage add variety to the design.

For your Christmas earrings, use a cluster of holly berries on a background of small leaves like Darwin barberry or malpighia to express the symbols of the season (Fig. 46e). Tiny bells may be added. Hang them on thread so they will move. Add sparkle if desired and a matching hair spray of berries and foliage with a wisp of red net or veiling.

You can make your own earring frame with a piece of 24-gauge wire long enough to start at the center front lobe of the ear, curve around the back, and up into the hair for 1½ inches. Cover wire with tape. Attach two flowers to fit over front of ear. Cover rest of frame

FIG. 46b   FIG. 46c   FIG. 46d

FIG. 46e   FIG. 46f   FIG. 46g   FIG. 46h

FIG. 46i   FIG. 46j   FIG. 46k

with satin ribbon. Finish with a knot at top and ribbon cut on a slant (Fig. 46f). Any small flowers are suitable for this design.

A single fuchsia blossom hanging like a bell is chic (Fig. 46g). Use thread and needle technique or very fine wire to fasten flower securely to the base. Or wire a silver braid bow to the frame, attach a dainty bleeding heart by fine wire or thread so it moves gently as it dangles (Fig. 46h).

Hyacinth blossoms or tuberoses (with part of tube removed) dangling down from the ear are charming for evening wear. Use thread-and-needle procedure to string and attach to frame (Fig. 46i). A tiny ball of moist cotton inserted in the flower insures freshness. For a glamorous teardrop design, use lily-of-the-valley florets, touch the edges ever so lightly with glue, and sprinkle with glitter.

For a larger base for dangle earrings, use a small hair clip. Pad the ends with cotton to prevent pinching, then cover clip with tape. Attach a tiny corsage of garden gems to the clip. Small, double azalea blooms with own foliage can be used (Fig. 46j).

Try the lei technique with tiny flowers. Tubular epidendrum orchid blooms are selected for illustration. String blossoms on a matching thread, using a long needle. Arrange in a loop and tie at top, attaching to earring base. Glue three tiny blossoms or one round bloom, as a ranunculus, to center circle of frame (Fig. 46k).

FLORAL ACCENTS

You will find it fun to duplicate the jewelry trends of the season in flower designs. Charming little floral "scatter pins" are effective when in style. Since pockets are always in vogue, they offer a suitable place for flowers. Experiment with a loose spray of feathered carnations pinned above the pocket and a matching handkerchief tucked in it. Or make little twin corsages for identical pockets. Floral buttons are gay highlights for a spring suit and are made by gluing the flowers to bone or plastic button bases. Make your initial of flowers and wear it on your lapel.

A narrow shoulder strap on an evening gown calls for a corsage of equal size. Use sweetheart roses in a single line with appropriate bows on the ends.

A full net scarf around the shoulders may have a single scabiosa, anemone or hydrangea fastened at the knot. Some of the new dark hydrangeas are effective in the garden and on the costume.

Use a belt of flowers if you have a very simple dress and a slender waist. A spray type design with trailing buds and loops of ribbon is good on a feminine dress. If a narrow velvet ribbon is used for a belt, sew a few dainty watsonias or hyacinths to the ends of the bow tie.

Purse designs are effective for parties. Abutilon (flowering maple) is delicate. Lovely blue agapanthus (lily of the Nile) or yellow spray orchids show up well on a brown satin bag, and alstroemerias in white and pink look well on black.

A word of warning is in order, lest you are too enthusiastic about floral accents. Remember that any corsage is a costume accessory. It must be in complete harmony with the costume and a definite part of it. These various suggestions are fascinating to make up, but do not overdo. Too many floral accents spoil the effect. When in doubt, don't. But do not be afraid to try new ideas. Test them on your family and close friends. If their reaction is good, you can wear your designs in public with confidence.

CORSAGES FOR JUNIORS

Corsages for the very young and the subdebs should be made of flowers and designs suitable to the size and age of the wearer.

The tiny miss will love to have two or three fresh flowers fastened to her hair ribbon. Arrange a matching flower basket for her to take to her friend for a birthday present. To do this, place ½ inch square mesh wire in the basket and place flower stems down inside the wire, beginning at the center and working out to the edges. Wild flowers, dried seed pods, and cones are close at hand for youngsters at summer camps.

Recital flowers for the very young should be in a design to be carried, rather than worn, so they will not interfere with her movements during the performance. Make a miniature reticule of net, and cover it with sweetheart roses.

Lollipop corsages make clever party favors for the kindergarten set. Choose lollipops wrapped in cellophane. Bind 3 or 5 together by wiring around the sticks. Make clusters of popcorn, cover wire with white floral tape and add to the lollipops. Finish with checkered hair ribbon bow. Gum drops wrapped in cellophane or hard candies in colored foil can make a child's wreath corsage with a tiny bow with streamers at one side.

Taped wire loops shaped into a fan with a corsage attached at the base make an attractive favor for a little girls' party.

A small hair clip will anchor a very small flower corsage instead of a pin, either in the hair or on a dress. A pair of tiny corsages is enchanting on a pretty little girl.

The very young can cover a rubber jar ring with tufts of evergreen and a bow, the edges of the leaves flecked with white shoe polish and sprinkled with sparkles while wet. Older children can create designs by gluing tiny seed pods and cones onto plastic pins from the dime store.

The junior high girl will enjoy a nosegay to carry to a party, or a pair of chain bracelets made in the lei technique.

The sophisticated subdebs like to make their own corsages, and they favor off-the-shoulder designs.

Boutonnieres

When you select flowers for your own corsage, also choose a blossom for your escort. Favorites for men are a small red floribunda rose, a small red camellia, chrysanthemum, carnation (pull calyx down), cornflower, Grand Duke jasmine, fleur d'amour, pompom aster, narcissus, or small vanda orchids. Wire properly by the piercing, clutch, or hook procedure, depending on strength of flower head, tape, and attach a $1\frac{1}{4}$- to 2-inch pin for use on back of lapel. Ushers for weddings, churches, and concerts usually wear a boutonniere. Why not extend the habit to organization heads, executives, salesmen, chairmen of social events, and speakers at political meetings? Men's Garden Club officers could set the pace, and don't forget a boutonniere for Father's Day.

PLATE VIII

Material: Sweetheart roses, *Leucocoryne ixioides,* native orchids (*Calopogon pulchellus*).

Form: Circular.

Line: Semi-concentric with triangle of roses in the center.

Color harmony: Analogous—pink, orchid, blue.

Texture: Fussy, fine.

Finishing: Pearl necklace, orchid floral tape.

Technique:

Wire each rose individually by pushing a 6-inch length of 28-gauge wire through the calyx and straightening under the flower. Make a loose triangle of the roses and bind the stems tightly together at one point as shown in Fig. VIII.3.

Shorten the stems of the tiny leucocorynes and orchids to ½ inch. Place a wisp of moist cotton around the stems to protect them and keep flowers from wilting. Use fine hair wire, 32-gauge, in 5-inch lengths, twisting half of it tightly around the cotton-covered stems. Cover the single wire stem with orchid or pink floral tape (**Fig. VIII.1**).

Make the little flowers into small groups by taping together one by one with little strips of floral tape (**Fig. VIII.2**). Arrange the little

PLATE VIII

Necklace Ornament of Sweetheart Roses and Native Orchids

groups around the triangle of roses in the center (Fig. VIII.3). Bind all stems together at assembly point and cut stems off short.

If a high necked dress is worn, pin corsage to dress and necklace. For a low or strapless dress, attach corsage to necklace with plastic-coated wire, or stick to skin with Scotch tape or jewelry glue.

Nearly 2 dozen little flowers comprise this composition, which is a challenging design. The tiny flowers in pastel colors with pearls are reminiscent of the Victorian era.

Corsage by: Mrs. Edward A. Hall.

PLATE IX

Fig. IX.1   Fig. IX.2

Material: Camellias.

Form: Circular.

Line: Zigzag line of blossoms about a central camellia.

Color harmony: Analogous—white, pink, and rose.

Texture: Waxy and wavy.

Finishing: Pink net, pink and rose satin ribbon.

Technique:

Seven variegated Hermes camellias are used for this dainty and fanciful spring bonnet. Wire each camellia with cross wires through the lower petals as described in Chapter IV. Tape wires with pink, orchid, or white floral tape.

76

PLATE IX

Pink Hermes Camellias in a Net Cloud

Make two circles of wire, one 4 inches and another 6½ inches in diameter. Tape and cover with pink satin ribbon. Fasten circles together with tape as shown in Fig. IX.1. Span the smaller circle with four thicknesses of pink net. Cut surplus from edges. Catch net at intervals about the wire circle with needle and thread.

Make seven ruffles of pink net by shirring with needle and thread or running a wire through the lower edge and gathering into a circle. Place a camellia in each circle of net for softness, and pull the ruffle tight around the stem.

Sew center camellia to base. Sew remaining flowers around it. Sew in little loops of pink and rose satin where needed (Fig. IX.2). Use a few bobby pins to hold hat secure on the head.

Hat by: Mrs. Herman Haefle.

IX

CORSAGES WITHOUT FLOWERS

The modern corsage takes in a much wider variety of material than flowers alone, just as it is worn many places other than the left shoulder. Other favorite corsage ingredients are dried materials (seed pods, cones, nuts, and grasses), fresh fruit, and feathers.

Dried Materials

Collecting and making corsages of dried materials is a fascinating hobby in itself. The corsages are not only attractive, but practical. The crisp winter things are durable, and are especially appropriate for wear on days when cold winds would play havoc with delicate flowers. Besides, the dried things are available when the garden is snowbound, or they can be harvested in the fall and stored away until needed.

Here is a whole new field of colors and textures. Although most of the dried materials are in shades of brown, the analogous harmonies made by careful combinations can be symphonies. Textures include smooth acorns, fuzzy pussy willows, prickly sweet gum balls, and feathery grasses. The sepals of a magnolia grandiflora blossom feel like undressed kid. Notice the marvelous textures in the corsage shown in Plate X.

Take care that the texture of the fresh or dried material is carried out in the ribbon. Cellophane bows are appropriate when a slick surface is wanted to harmonize with kumquats or peppers, and rough woven ribbons give a coarse accent with cone flowers, wheat, or tangerines.

Cones of all sizes are in demand, from the very petite alder cones to the large ones several inches in circumference. They are used whole, or in horizontal or vertical sections. There is even a place for individual scales. Pointed Siberian iris pods, round cranberries, and twisted bauhinia pods are interesting.

The designs of the dried corsages are adaptations of the basic ones used for flowers. Large forms make the "flowers," small pointed items are used as "buds," and the unusual broad pods represent leaves. A good "foliage" choice is the jacaranda pod cut into halves, for it has exquisite interior design.

When practical the dried items are wired like flowers, but some require special techniques. They are generally easier to work with than fresh flowers, as they are sturdier, and are especially recommended for practice items by the beginning corsage hobbyist.

FIG. 47   FIG. 48

Pods with no stems (gladiolus) are wired by pushing 26-gauge wire through the base of the pod, as in Fig. 47a. With acorns, eucalyptus, and other solid pods, it is necessary to pierce them first with a sharp tool (Fig. 47b). Then wire as usual, pushing wire all the way through and pulling down underneath for a double stem. Circle a cone with wire just above the lowest row of scales, as in Fig. 48. Pull the wire tight to the center of the cone and bring it down beneath the scales to make the stem. Pieces of pine and cedrus cones are wired the same way. Twenty-four-gauge wire is generally used for these heavy items.

Cones may be glamourized by being placed in a warm oven until the pitch runs over the surface. Be sure to use an old pan, and leave the oven door open a crack so you can watch them, because they scorch quickly.

Cones that are too bulky for artistic use may be cut crosswise into flat cone flowers. Slice off the top and bottom. The top offers one pattern, the up-turned bottom another. If the cone is large, cut the center section into additional slices. A big cone may provide 6 or 7 "flowers." Use a small saw or pruner for the first cut, and then trim the scales on each piece until you have the desired shape. The open flower forms may be used as the center of interest like you would use roses or daisies, and smaller pointed cones or pods added for accent just like buds.

FIG. 49   FIG. 50

The English version of the cone flower is to cut a small pine cone in half vertically instead of horizontally (Fig. 49). This makes a beautiful tree-like section. Use four halves, wiring individually around the lower scales. Place small cones, ivy or cistus pods in the center, and put the four "petals" around it. Assemble tightly under the flower head and tape the stems all at once. Additional cone halves may be used for buds if needed to complete the design.

Many dried things come in flower-shaped forms. Cotton sepals are readymade, the tops of some cones are perfect roses, and a persimmon calyx is a unique blossom. Hawaiian wood roses look like parchment flowers, but they are really morning-glory seed pods.

Create your own winter flowers by making petals of scales of cedrus deodara, individually wired and placed around "stamens" of tiny azalea seed pods or hemlock cones (Fig. 50).

Rye grass heads from the field and grains such as oats, wheat and rice, and tiny seeded sprays from the roadside can be included to lighten the appearance of a corsage and to emphasize the subtle color harmonies. Other dried materials, with wiring instructions and suggestions for use, are given in the Appendix charts at the end of the book.

FRUITS AND BERRIES

Fruits and berries are excellent material for tailored corsages and comprise another source for winter decor. Fruits from tiny button size on up may be used, but care should be taken that the corsage is not too heavy.

Fruit corsages may be made in any design that adapts gracefully to the form of the material, but the circular design illustrated by the holly corsage, Plate XI, is the most popular.

Small fruits like privet, snowberries, jasmine, madroña, mountain-ash, skimmia, pyracantha, and ardisia are wired like small sprigs of flowers. Hook the wire up into the cluster and twist around the stem (Fig. 14). Clear shellac (or orange shellac for an antiqued effect) tends to make some berries and fruits last longer. Wire single fruits—crabapples, kumquats, lady apples, limes, as in Fig. 11. Push a short guide wire up into the fruit before attaching the long wire stem. To hold wire in fruit, drop a little Ducco cement into the hole.

Experiment also with little red and green peppers, bayberries, and bittersweet.

A collarette of foliage is an excellent foil for berries, and its choice offers a challenge. Use variegated dracaena foliage with white jasmine berries. Red autumn leaves are good with red berries to complete a warm analogy. Dubonnet pernettya berries make a contrasting harmony with chartreuse pothos leaves. If you live in a cold climate, choose your house plants with the idea of snipping an occasional leaf for your winter corsages. Suitable are the round white-edged leaves of aralia, glossy philodendron leaves, and the interesting dieffenbachias, which can be cut to size (see Plate V). Single scales of large pine cones may be substituted for foliage, combining the arts of making dried and fruit corsages.

FEATHERS

The feather art, long practiced by the Indians, has found a counterpart in the modern corsage craft, and masterpieces of feathers are to be seen at flower shows and county fairs.

The Northwest Indians have easy access to pheasants, quail, grouse, mallard, and owl feathers. The rural corsage hobbyist can use chicken, turkey, or duck plumage. If there is not a huntsman in the family, the city artist can buy her materials at the dime or millinery supply store.

Until you have wired and taped and fashioned individual feathers into feather flowers, you have not fully enjoyed the many facets of corsage craft. Tantalizing creations can be made from mottled, barred. splashed and dotted feathers, especially those with an iridescent quality.

The pheasant corsage is among the most striking. The creamy feathers with speckled throats, narrow reddish-brown borders and leaf-like markings make beautiful five-petal flowers (Fig. 51).

Group your feathers for size. Select those about an inch or an inch and a half in length. Strip the little fuzzy feathers from the bottom. Wrap the tiny ends with 32-gauge wire and allow about 3 inches of wire for the stem. Twenty-five feathers will be needed for a five-flower corsage. Gather five evenly marked and harmonious feathers together and place them about little jeweled or chenille stamens (available at dime store for making artificial flowers). Readjust until a perfect flower is formed. Tape securely well up under the head.

This same technique is used with other feathers. Make a spectacular white evening corsage of capon feathers. If you wish color accent, use red tape, bow, and stamens.

Wrapped in Cellophane

Cellophane "peach blossoms" or "violets" make a festive party corsage when fresh flowers are not available.

The "peach blossoms" are made of kernels of corn. Cut pink cellophane into 1½-inch squares, and cut the squares in half crosswise. Wrap each kernel in cellophane as shown in Fig. 52. Wire at the base, allowing a 3-inch stem. Gather five of the kernels around artificial stamens, wire the stems together, and tape. The little flower looks like a glistening spring bloom. Assemble the blossoms into a spray design.

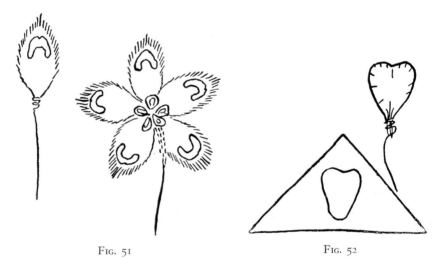

FIG. 51   FIG. 52

The "violet" corsage is made in the same manner, using pumpkin seeds and purple cellophane. Use yellow stamens, and then gather the "violets" into a bunch and surround with foliage.

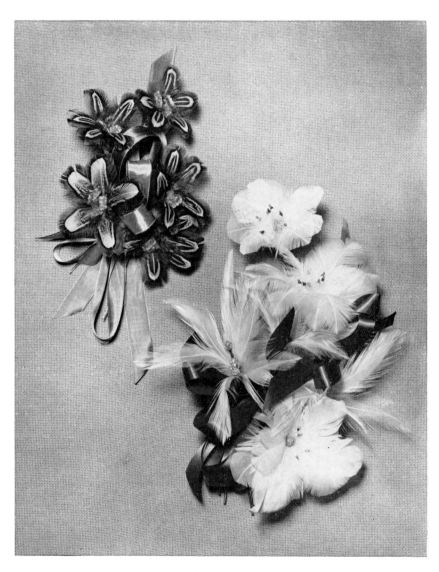

Pheasant Corsage by Mrs. C. F. Hill
White Capon Corsage by Mrs. George Henderson

PLATE X

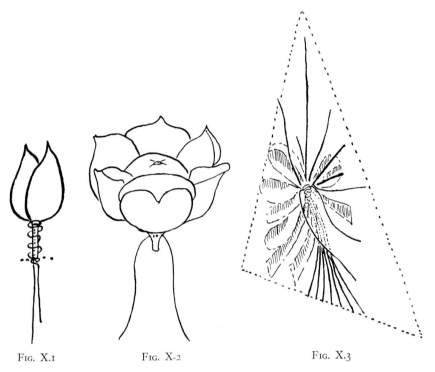

FIG. X.1   FIG. X-2   FIG. X.3

Material: *Ipomoea tuberosa* or Hawaiian wood roses, *Argyreia nervosa* or wood cherries or miniature wood roses, and *Bixa orellana* or lipstick pods.

Form: Triangle.

Line: Slight curve from the pointed pods at the top, through center blossom and lower rose. Spherical rose centers are repeated by spherical cherry centers.

Texture: Fuzzy pods, satin rose petals, suede cherry sepals.

Color harmony: Muted tones of gray, beige, brown, and dull red.

Finishing: Two kinds of ribbon, brown satin and chartreuse picoted with brown. Stems cut on a slant.

Technique:

Wire each lipstick pod and each of the small wooden cherries by simply twisting a 14-inch length of 26-gauge wire well around the ½-inch stem and pulling the ends down straight (Fig. X.1).

86

PLATE X

Triangle of Wood Roses, Wood Cherries, and Lipstick Pods

Pierce the wood roses through the thick stem just under the head. Push a 26-gauge wire through half its length, twist it about the stem several times and straighten ends (Fig. X.2).

After individual parts are taped, assemble according to Fig. X.3. Start with the pointed pods at the top, add the open blossom, then the small cherries, and finally the second rose which is bent back on itself. The assembly point is under the top rose. Cover assembly wire with tape.

Add the rich two-toned ribbon bow with contrasting textures to complete the triangular pattern.

Corsage by: Glad Reusch.

PLATE XI

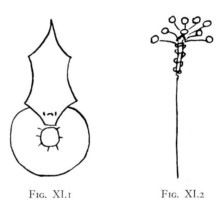

Fɪɢ. XI.1   Fɪɢ. XI.2

Material: Holly berries and leaves
Form: Circular.
Line: Wheel spokes and hub.
Texture: Smooth leaves and berries, accented with a tinseled edge.
Color harmony: Contrasting—red and green.
Finishing: Red satin ribbon bow and scrolled stem.
Technique:

Brush the holly leaves on the edges with colorless nail polish, mucilage, or egg white and sprinkle immediately with mirror metallics.

Staple or sew six holly leaves to a gardenia collar (Fig. XI.1 and Fig. 15). Cut off the stems and lower edges of the leaves if necessary to keep the design flat and uniform.

PLATE XI

Circle of Holly Berries and Tinsel-edged Leaves

Wire several bunches of berries together into one bunch with a long 18-inch length of 26-gauge wire (Fig. XI.2). Add two more pieces of wire for thickness, tape wires their full length, and cover with red satin ribbon. Pull through the collar and twist end into a scroll. The scroll is decorative and helps to stabilize the corsage when it is worn.

Complete with a full bow of red satin ribbon tied around central stem under gardenia collar. Ten or twelve loops and about half as many ends are needed to fill in the circular form.

Corsage by: Miss Nettie Carlson.

X

BOUQUETS

There is an old Chinese proverb which says, "Habits and customs differ, but all peoples have the love of flowers in their hearts." The significance of this proverb is apparent on special occasions, for flowers are an integral part of weddings, parties, and other festive events.

Bouquets are large floral arrangements, designed to be carried. Basically the construction principles are the same as those for corsages: conditioning, wiring, and taping the individual flowers before assembling them into a pleasing design.

There are three groups in which bouquet designs may be classed: colonial, cascade, and modern.

The Colonial

The symmetrical nosegay or colonial bouquet is a favorite of long standing. Although variations have come through the years, the dainty collarette around concentric rings of pastel flowers is still held in special affection. Miniature designs of the colonial are used for corsages and were mentioned in Chapter VI. Construction of the colonial bouquet is along the same lines, although the volume of material involved makes it more complicated.

The colonial pictured in Plate XII is the ultimate in technique, form, and color. The sketches illustrate the technique for preparing a colonial of four rows around a center flower. All individual flowers or tiny groups are wired with 26- or 28-gauge wire, depending upon their weight. Fig. 53a shows the approximate length wire for each row. Each row is progressively longer than the one before, but only sufficient to reach the center and be secured. It is not necessary to tape individual stems, as the flowers are so close together no wires show.

The center rosebud is wired with heavy 24-gauge wire which serves as the upright on which the construction is based. Surround the rose completely with the flowers of the innermost row. Place 3 flowers in position, then bind to rose stem with fine wire. Add 3 more the same way until flower is surrounded (Fig. 53b). Place the following rows 1 by 1 and wire the same way. Finally cut the ends off on a slant, twist together firmly as in Fig. 53c, and cover with tape. Slip a lace, maline, or net collar over the stems, back with a stiff paper collar to hold up the lace, and add ribbon. The result is a perfectly balanced design (Fig. 53d).

The colonial may be made of flowers of one kind or color. Where more than one color is used, each row should be distinct. For example, start with a red rosebud, raised high. Circle with a row of white, then blue, yellow, lavender, and pink flowers. Those suitable for a mixed colonial include:

> white—feverfew, mock orange, button chrysanthemum, lemon blossom, orange blossom, oleander;
>
> blue—delphinium florets, cornflower, forget-me-not;
>
> yellow—carnation petals, chrysanthemum, narcissus, primrose;
>
> lavender—ageratum, stock florets, sweet pea;
>
> pink—bouvardia, rose daphne, carnation petals, button chrysanthemum, sweet pea, oleander.

Dainty foliages are ideal for the outer edge to preserve the light, airy effect characteristic of the colonial design.

Instead of a variety of small flowers, a few large blossoms of one kind and color such as double hollyhocks, open roses, or tuberous begonias may be used in a colonial design. Place one blossom in the center and 6 or more uniformly sized and colored flowers in a circle around it, as in Fig. 54. Make a collar of satin ribbon that is 4 inches wide, and attach loops of the same ribbon below the collar. This style is especially suitable for bridesmaids.

For a holiday party, a debutante may choose a colonial of white chrysanthemums, red roses, holly berries, and holly leaves surrounded by a pleated red maline ruffle.

A beautiful white colonial is made of flattened Easter lily petals for the collarette, with valley lilies or stephanotis in the center.

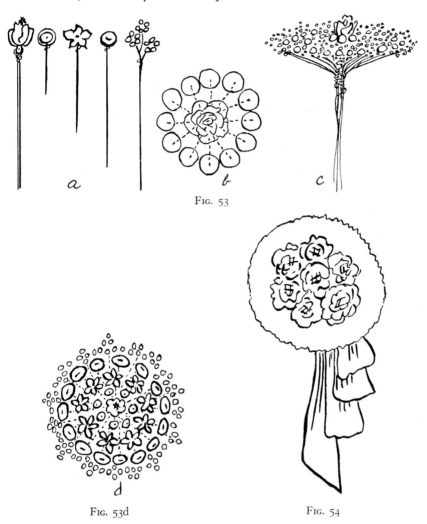

FIG. 53

FIG. 53d   FIG. 54

CASCADE BOUQUETS

The triangular shaped cascade bouquet is a very popular type of design, and is illustrated with gladioli and tuberoses in Plate XIII. The wide part of the triangle is at the top, and the long sides trail to a narrow point about 15 or 20 inches from the center of the design.

In assembling the cascade bouquet, the important thing is to keep it as light as possible. Wire each flower individually with wire as fine as is consistent with its weight. Then tape each flower and assemble with tape as described in Chapter VI. If more than one cascade is used, make the central part of the bouquet first, then make the cascades separately and attach securely under the focal point.

Ivy, smilax, euonymus, and wandering jew are graceful foliage choices for a trailing design.

THE MODERN BOUQUET

The connotation of the word "modern" brings to mind the stylized, bold type of flower. These flowers and their foliages are so dominant that only a few are needed, and hence the modern bouquet designs have evolved.

The flowers that do well in modern designs include: anthurium, strelitzia, spathyphyllum, cattleya orchid, cypripedium, parrot tulip, carnation, camellia, gardenia, gloriosa, spider chrysanthemum, gladiolus, and calla.

Gloriosas are suitable for the cascade form of the wide-topped triangle. About 2 dozen flowers are required. A few flame gerberas may complement the gloriosas at the center of interest. Try this also with croton and ivy, without flowers.

A dramatic effect is the use of a large satin-covered circle on which is mounted a long train of white gladiolus reaching nearly to the hemline, shown in Fig. 55. A large portion of the circle is visible, the flowers being placed to one side, and a few smaller flowers tucked on the opposite side. Maintain a width of about 9 inches through the upper part of the bouquet and taper the ends. Loops of wide ribbon may be added among the top blossoms.

The crescent form, with the ends turned up or down, and the epaulet form with a central cascade, are effective bouquets.

The muff is built on the rectangular form. The muff itself, of cotton rolls, is covered with wide satin ribbon, plain or shirred. Make a corsage of bold blossoms (perhaps speciosum alba lilies) and pin it to one side. The sketch, Fig. 56, features tulips and pointed tulip foliage. The petals of one blossom are rolled back for emphasis, and an extra blossom tied where the ribbon is knotted on the end. With some flowers, gold ribbon is effective for the muff covering. Blended roses of yellow, saffron, and orange are rich in color, and may be used with gold net leaves. Corsages suitable for muffs may also be used on pocketbooks.

FIG. 55   FIG. 56   FIG. 57

The muff may be made of flowers by covering the satin base solidly. If carnations are used, pull back the calyx of each flower to fluff out the petals. Wire individually as in Fig. 12, tape, and sew to muff or assemble first with tape. A solid foundation of chrysanthemums may be accented with a corsage of bold lilies. A muff of shaggy or spider chrysanthemums looks like ostrich plumes.

The fan form has a variety of designs. Single ribs may be composed of small flowers, or a basic wire frame covered with net ruffles may have a spray corsage at the apex. A variation of the fan shape for the wedding party is shown in Fig. 57. Make a shield of net over an oval wire frame about 18 by 12 inches. Place several stalks of gladioli against it and tie at the handle with a wide ribbon bow.

Other good bouquet combinations are: white althaea or hollyhock and annual babysbreath; daisies with larkspur; lilacs and open tulips; laceflowers, iris and rubrum lilies; phalaenopsis orchids, lilies, and caladium foliage.

Since a bouquet is so big, it is especially important that color, form, and texture be carefully considered. Compare flowers and costume before you begin construction to be sure the colors are absolutely harmonious, and the textures agreeable. Remember, too, that blue, dark purple, and yellow fade out under artificial light, and the effectiveness of the bouquet is lost if these colors are selected for evening events.

Experiment with different flowers and designs, as the flowers will adapt to one design more readily than another. If the appearance of the bouquet is stiff, try another design until you find one to which the flowers seem suited. Take care, also, that the result has a light, airy appearance, and does not look bulky or heavy.

PLATE XII

Fig. XII.1

Material: All white flowers. Rose, allium, rosebuds, stock, azalea buds.
Maidenhair fern for foliage note

Form: Circular.

Line: Concentric circles.

Color harmony: Predominantly white.

Texture: Smooth rose petals, fussy small flowers, and fern.

Finishing: Chantilly lace colonial collar. Narrow satin and lace streamers.

Technique:

This bouquet in the colonial tradition has extraordinary charm.
The technique for making a colonial is given in detail in the text of
this chapter. Briefly, proceed as follows:

Wire and tape the individual flowers with white floral tape down
just 1 inch under flower head. (For wire gauge and length, see text
and Fig. 53a.) Raise the central rose high. Surround it with a delicate
circle of tiny allium blossoms. Wire each few stems tightly to the
rose stem. Insert the third row of white rosebuds evenly about the
allium. Make the intermittent fourth row of stock florets. Complete
the picture with pointed white azalea buds (Fig. XII.1). Add little
wired sprigs of maidenhair fern for softness and contrast. Sew a
chantilly lace ruffle to a paper lace collar and pull into place under
flowers.

PLATE XII

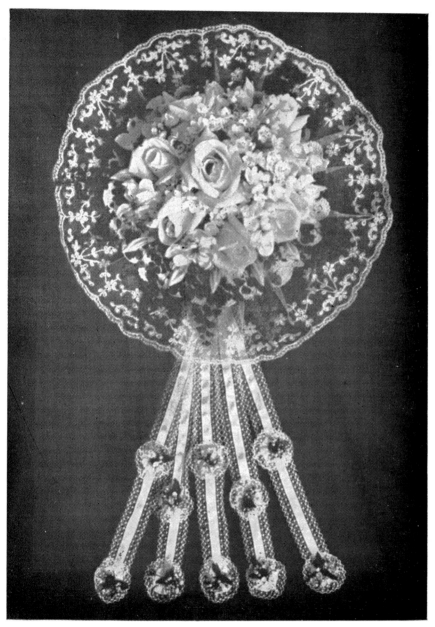

White Colonial Bouquet of Roses and Buds, Allium, Stock, Azalea Buds, and
Maidenhair Fern

Design the shower of ribbon streamers of narrow white satin with tiny lace sewed to the ribbon edge. (Streamers are spread in the photograph but actually hang gracefully and may be any length desired.) Gather little circles of ribbon and lace to make backgrounds for the tiny spirea flowers sewed to them. Attach streamers with wire to the wire handle of the bouquet.

Make the handle by twisting the wire stems together, covering them with tape and then with satin ribbon.

Bouquet by: Mrs. W. Leroy MacGowan.

PLATE XIII

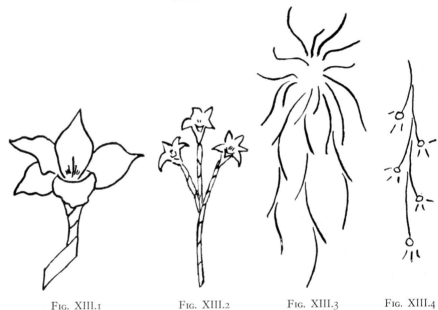

FIG. XIII.1   FIG. XIII.2   FIG. XIII.3   FIG. XIII.4

Material: Gladioli and tuberoses.
Form: Cascade.
Line: Circular with trailing curves.
Texture: Smooth gladioli petals, waxy tuberoses, stiff, lacy ribbon.
Color harmony: Monochromatic—all white.
Finishing: Wide loops of illusion ribbon.
Technique:

This charming 30-inch cascade bouquet shows smart designing. Remove the green calyx from the individual gladioli blossoms. Tape

PLATE XIII

Cascade of Gladioli and Tuberoses

the base of the flower for protection with white tape, push 26-guage wire through tape, straighten ends, and tape again (Fig. XIII.1). Prepare each tuberose the same way, but use finer 28- or 30-gauge wire. The length of wire used is determined by the design and the construction. Tuberoses added singly are taped to the end of the stem. If, however, you gather three tuberoses together to facilitate assembling as in this design, then each wire is taped only 2 inches and is completely covered as one stem is attached to the next with white floral tape (Fig. XIII.2).

Starting with the circular movement in the center, place the gladioli closely at the focal point and scatter a few blossoms about the edge of the circle (Fig. XIII.3). Insert tuberoses where needed to complete the design of the central circle.

Make the three cascades separately (Fig. XIII.4), and attach the end of each to the center section securely under the focal point. Since each blossom is taped to the previous one with white tape, there are no exposed wires and the design is light and airy. Make the center cascade longer than the other two. About two dozen gladioli florets and five or six dozen tuberoses are required for this design.

Use loops of illusion ribbon of equal size, and tuck them in deftly to emphasize the circular form, securing to frame with wire.

Bouquet by: Mrs. Edwin Linwood Thomas.

XI

AROUND THE CALENDAR

Since flowers are always appropriate, there are corsage designs suitable to every month and special event of the year. The speed of air express makes it possible to bring blossoms from other parts of the world in "tree-ripened freshness" when they are not available at home. So now the entire plant kingdom is at the command of the corsage hobbyist.

JANUARY

The New Year theme adapts easily to corsage designs that are suitable for the season's festivities. Here are some suggestions: a white carnation muff, with the numerals of the new year added in flowers of another color; a corsage of feathered red carnations on a bell-shaped frame of chenille or tape, and for the gong a tiny parchment scroll on which resolutions are neatly written. To any corsage add a few small crystalline snowballs or a tiny horn and champagne glass on narrow ribbons.

FEBRUARY

Valentine's Day calls for red roses, red chenille hearts, and red satin bows. A lace collar is in keeping, too. Make a flower by reversing the petals of a hibiscus, wiring each separately with the dark center at outer edge and lighter color in middle. Arrange five petals together around a tiny flower of contrasting color. See Fig. 40b for a heart-shaped frame for a holiday corsage.

March

St. Patrick's Day and the "wearin' of the green" are observed by green clover and dyed green carnations. A dominantly green cymbidium may have the color emphasized by green ribbon. A green silk miniature harp instead of a flower, backed with green foliage, is smart. The harp base is fashioned as in Fig. 40.

April

The purity of the Easter season is best expressed with lilies. Try a "Royal Flare" of a bunch of violets surrounded by Easter lily petals, flattened out and wired separately. An all-white variation of this design is the same collarette with a white peony or gardenia in the center. The bowknot of tiny white narcissus, Plate XIV, is a lovely springtime design.

A bunny may be made of three sections of white carnation. In one, place a piece of triangular pink chenille to represent the mouth and make two circles for eyes in the other sections of the flower. Ears are made of pink chenille covered with net. Tuck a nice bow under the chin, add pink chenille whiskers, three to each side.

May

A small corsage makes a delightful decoration atop a gift box and is especially appropriate for Mother's Day. She probably prefers miniature spring blooms, lilacs, and other old-fashioned favorites that are reminiscent of grandmother's garden. If the gift is a lace handkerchief, pin the corsage directly to it.

June

June is the month of roses. A wide choice from tiny to large in floribundas, polyanthas, and hybrid teas is available for the designer. The many forms, sizes, and colors make the designs almost unlimited. Buds or spray flowers used with roses help prevent the design from being monotonous. If roses are all of one size, take several petals, placed one on top of the other, and roll into a bud, or make a "sweetpea" out of two petals as in Fig. 21c for contrast with round forms.

JULY

Finding red, white, and blue for a patriotic corsage is a challenge, particularly the blue. Fortunately, ribbon may be used for one of the colors. In the reds we have roses, carnations, anemones, and tuberous begonias. The whites are stock, Esther Reed daisies, pieris floribunda, tuberoses, mockorange, feverfew, gladioli, and Dutch iris. Cornflowers, Perry blue Siberian iris, and deep delphinium florets provide the blue. Another way to achieve the color scheme is by wearing a red hibiscus or an epaulet of red verbena, geraniums, or ixora on a blue suit with a white blouse.

AUGUST

In the intense heat of the late summer, corsages should express coolness. Bluish-green succulents are ideal. A wide choice of colors is available in strawflowers (Helichrysum). They last well if picked when the blossoms are just opening. For a bon-voyage gift, tuck a purse-size flacon of perfume into a hibiscus corsage. A chatelaine type corsage can be made of two or three blooms. String tiny seeds for the connecting chain and allow the short ends of the chain to hang down.

SEPTEMBER

Dahlias and zinnias foretell the beginning of fall with their yellow, orange, and red hues. Leaves, too, are beginning to show tints of autumn, and combinations of late flowers with dried materials (grasses, sea oats, and pods) lead into the winter designs.

OCTOBER

The Halloween orange and black are provided by orange chrysanthemums, black liriope berries, and black satin ribbon bows. If black berries are not available, use orange pyracantha berries. Bittersweet, yellow crabapples and orange arctotis combined express the autumn spirit.

NOVEMBER

The harvest season is represented by using vegetables, wheat, oats, pheasant feathers, tiny fruits, and any flowers that are available. Don't combine all in one corsage. The pheasant feathers dictate the color of the flowers to be used with them, probably purple chrysanthemums. Wheat and oats harmonize with flowers on the warm side of the color wheel. Chestnuts, peanuts, cranberries, grain, and grasses combine to express the season. Use raffia or raveled rope for a bow.

DECEMBER

Red berries with glittering leaves are for gaiety, and the dried cones and seed pods may be touched with gold on the edges for the holiday season. For a conversational note, add tiny tinkling bells or a plastic snowman to a corsage. The Christmas rose (*Helleborus niger*) is very fitting for this season, for a legend tells that these waxy star-shaped flowers led the way to the Manger. A group of Christmas balls brightened with sparkles may serve as the focal point in a corsage, with seed pods, foliage, or angel feathers added and sprayed for the desired color effect.

SPECIAL EVENTS

A pair of dainty colonial corsages, one large and one small, are attractive gifts for a mother and her new baby daughter. Other hospital patients will appreciate a corsage to be pinned to the pillow, or a wristlet that may be worn and seen. Flowers with faint fragrance are desirable for pillow corsages, but not those that are overpowering like gardenias.

Small corsages and boutonnieres at each place decorate a party table and make attractive favors for the guests.

You will find that corsages may be adapted to any purpose where flowers, a gift, or an expression of friendship are in order.

PLATE XIV

Fig. XIV.1   Fig. XIV.2

Material: Narcissus florets.

Form: Bowknot—double circles with trailing ends.

Line: Illusion of a single line tied into a bow.

Color harmony: Monochromatic.

Texture: Waxy, fragile.

Finishing: Tapering ends.

Technique:

Shorten floret to ½ inch because the less bulky the material the more delicate will be the final result. The closer the flowers adhere to the line design, the more symmetrical will be the loop. Tape the tiny floret to protect the delicate stem, or wrap the stem with a bit of moist cotton, before wiring. Use very fine hair wire, 30 or 32 gauge, in 5-inch lengths. Twist it about the stem close up under the flower head (Fig. XIV.1). Cover wire with white tape.

Assemble by taping or twisting one floret to the next until the desired length is attained. Make in four separate parts and join at the center by binding sections together with fine assembly wire. A few extra florets may be needed at the center to fill out the design (Fig. XIV.2).

PLATE XIV

Bowknot of Narcissus Florets

Cornflowers, delphinium or stock florets, strawflowers, Primula auricula, or fragrant mock orange blossoms are suitable for this design.

Corsage by: Mrs. Howard VanBuskirk.

XII

BEYOND THE GARDEN GATE

In the florist shop are found flowers that vary from those in the garden, because the standbys are flown in from all parts of the world. The favorite gladiolus, carnation, rose, and orchid are available to the trade at all seasons; and, with a wide territory on which to draw, there is almost no limit to the variety of flowers that the florist can secure for his designs.

The florist's "must" list of the top dozen in the dominant flowers includes:

anemone	lily —auratum
camellia	speciosum, rubrum, and
carnation	alba
chrysanthemum	calla
Dutch iris	Easter
gardenia	umbellatum
gerbera	orchid—white and purple
gladiolus	cattleya
	peony
	rose

Spray and small flowers serve as filler flowers, used to lighten or add interest to the design, vary the texture or color harmony. Buds, too, serve this purpose, but the florist seldom has access to them because nearly all of the flowers planned for the trade are counted and sized with too great regularity. Desirable small flowers are:

babysbreath (annual)	lily of the valley
bouvardia	stephanotis
cornflower	stock
delphinium	sweet pea
hyacinth	tuberose
lilac	violet

The aristocratic and modern-looking blossoms, most of them hot-house or tropical specimens are included in the exotics. However, the garden has many equally beautiful blooms, and ambitious gardeners are growing their own orchids, anthuriums, and hibiscus in small glass houses. The anthurium corsage in Plate XVII illustrates the technique for these modern flowers. Effective flowers for sophisticated designs are:

anthurium	spider lily
clivia	strelitizia (bird of paradise)
gloriosa	tuberous begonia
parrot tulip	waterlily
spathyphyllum	

Though the cattleya orchid is known to all, and the cymbidium and cypripedium (ladyslipper) generally available, the trade would do well to promote other varieties of orchids that are lovely in form and extremely long-lasting. The combination of small and large orchids, harmonious in color and form, is shown in Plate XVI. There are many species and spray orchids that are appropriate found in the following genera:

calanthe	phaius
dendrobium	phalaenopsis
odontoglossum	vanda
oncidium	

Among the foliages used by the florist are these favorites:

caladium   holly
Chinese evergreen, varie-   mistletoe
   gated   smilax
croton   spathyphyllum
huckleberry   wandering jew
ivy, plain and variegated

A distinct modern note is made with an accent of croton and spathyphyllum foliage. Holly and mistletoe are used during the holiday season, often with white chrysanthemums.

The multiple or created flower, a favorite of the florist, is called by
many names. The one usually heard is "Duchess," except when it is
made of gladiolus petals and is a "Glamellia." When large petals surround tiny flowers, collarette fashion, like lily petals around violets, the
form is called a "Royal Flare." The usual multiple flower is made of
many petals of a given flower circled about a central bud until the blossom is of the desired size. The Glamellia is illustrated in Plate VI.
Other flowers suitable for this technique are roses, lilies, tulips, and
gardenias.

The huge chrysanthemum and the carnation adapt easily to the shat-
tered or feathered bloom. Though it seems cruel to take a flower apart,
the individual petals last just as well out of water as the entire bloom,
and a feathered bloom makes a daintier corsage. The feathering procedure is described with carnations in Chapter IV. Likewise, the petals
of a large Turner chrysanthemum make an interesting new blossom.
In assembling, start with the stems that have only a few petals and use
in increasing size until the largest group of petals is placed at the center.

If possible, the florist will ask the customer for color, type, and fragrance preference so the corsage will be suitable and pleasing to the
wearer. Some scents are distasteful to certain people, while a gentle fragrance enhances the beauty of the corsage. Some florists spray the corsage ever so lightly with a good perfume, so the recipient will have a
pleasant sensation on opening the box. It is natural to smell a flower,
and a pleasure to meet a sweet odor.

Many florists prefer to use a single wire of a heavier gauge in preparing individual flowers instead of the double wire stem advocated in the preceding chapters. One end of a 9-inch wire is pushed into or through the calyx, or twisted around under the head. The remaining straight end forms the single stem (Fig. 58). This conserves wire, but is likely to be a little bulkier than the finer double length.

NOVELTIES

Advanced corsage hobbyists are learning some of the techniques for making a flower of one form from the petals of another flower. The "Gladorchid" does not have the prestige of a real orchid, but is a popular novelty.

Choose 2 large sized gladiolus florets. Select the 2 broadest petals to be paired for the wings of the orchid. Next, cut 3 narrow petals from 3 separate gladiolus petals. Finally choose one petal with a natural curve to be used for the trumpet (Fig. 59). If lavender gladiolus are used, fold a petal from a purple or magenta gladiolus inside the trumpet to represent the color in the throat of an orchid. Coleus leaves or

FIG. 58   FIG. 59   FIG. 60. Glad Butterfly

other flower petals may be used for this accent. Tape each petal with a tiny piece of tape. Use 32-gauge wire to bind each petal and cover with tape for 1 inch. Roll the trumpet petal, insert color, tape, wire and tape as above. Assemble by placing 1 narrow petal at the top, the 2 wings at the sides, two narrow petals at the bottom, and then the trumpet facing outward. Press the taped wires together, bind securely, and cover with tape.

The "Glad butterfly" is primarily used as a hair ornament. Select one gladiolus bud and two wing-like petals. The bud represents the body of the butterfly. Wire the wings as in Fig. 18, and run ends of the wire through the lower side of the body. Use gold wire cord for the antennae and modeling clay on wire for the eyes (Fig. 60).

To make a holiday flower ball, use a sphere of Styrofoam or a 2-inch ball of moss. Fill with holly berries and leaves. Sharpen stem tips to pierce the ball or wire the stems with a hairpin wire. Then double a long wire into a hairpin and run through the center of the sphere. Attach a bow at the bottom loop. Cut off surplus wire at top, and attach a bow and a 12-inch ribbon loop so ball can be carried on arm. Try this same idea with any flowers. Small yellow chrysanthemums and yellow bows are attractive.

PLATE XV

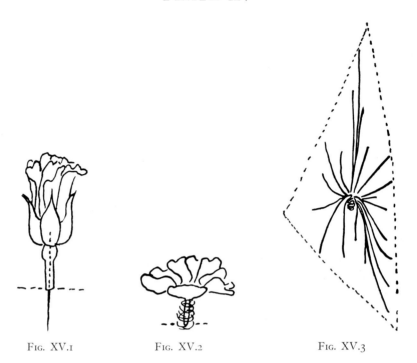

FIG. XV.1   FIG. XV.2   FIG. XV.3

Material: Pink rosebuds, deeper half open roses, wine stock, gray-green stock foliage.

Form Triangle.

Line: Perpendicular extension of buds and stock from focal point.

Color harmony: Analogous—pink, rose, wine.

Texture: Plain surface of rose petals and foliage contrasts with the fussy texture of the stock, woven ribbon, and crinkled edges of rosebud petals.

Finishing: Silver ribbon adds brilliance to the design and complements the silvery-green center of the stock.

Technique:

Reduce rose stems to ½ inch. Push a short 24-gauge guide wire up into the green calyx as shown in Fig. XV.1. Using a 14-inch length of wire caught at the halfway mark, twist it about the stem several times, pull ends down vertically and cover with tape. Allow the artistic sepal tips to remain if they fit the bud tightly.

PLATE XV

Triangle of Pink Roses and Buds with Wine-Red Stock

Cut stock stems to ½ inch. Place a wisp of moist cotton about the stem, twist wire over cotton as described above (Fig. XV.2). Straighten wire ends and tape.

Assemble the wired flowers as shown in the skeleton sketch, Fig. XV.3. The assembly point is directly under the lowest rose. As you add each additional blossom, bind tightly with 32-gauge wire at assembly point. Cover assembly wire with tape. Make a silver ribbon bow of various sized loops and tuck it in among the blossoms, tying to corsage skeleton at focal point. Note how a touch of ribbon at the top carries the eye into the design. Cut all wires off short on a slant so no stems show.

Corsage by: Mrs. W. Leroy MacGowan.

PLATE XVI

FIG. XVI.1   FIG. XVI.2

Material: Cattleya and dendrobium orchids.
Form: Hogarth curve.
Line: Reverse "S" curve.
Color harmony: Analogous.
Texture: Tissue paper, crinkly and waxy.
Finishing: Two-toned orchid ribbon and curved stems.
Technique:

Repetition in form and color highlights this orchid extravaganza. Cut the stems to 1 inch on the dendrobiums and about 2 inches on the cattleya and wire as shown in Fig. 9. Tape the dendrobium stems for protection (Fig. XVI.1). Bind wire over the tape and then completely cover the wire stem with lavender floral tape.

Using the large cattleya as the dominant bloom, place two of the small dendrobiums at the top and wire tightly to the cattleya stem. Arrange the remaining three dendrobiums below the large blossom in the drop method; that is, place the blossoms in position, double the stem back up to the assembly point under the cattleya, and fasten

PLATE XVI

Hogarth Curve of Cattleya and Dendrobium Orchids

securely with assembly wire (Fig. XVI.2). All blossoms face the same way for harmony. The position shown in the photograph is the proper way to wear an orchid. Notice that the lip faces out, so you can see into the flower.

Using heavy orchid and purple satin ribbon, make ribbon loops, tie to stems at assembly point and arrange loops to one side with curving ends to emphasize the lower curve of the Hogarth form. Note the importance of the curved stems and ribbon ends to complete the design.

Corsage by: Mrs. Bruno W. Alberts.

PLATE XVII

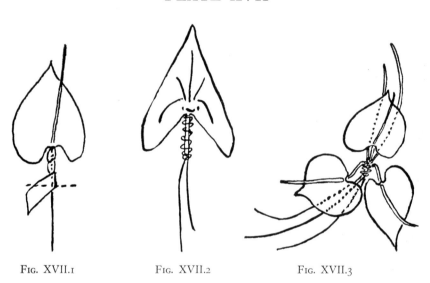

FIG. XVII.1   FIG. XVII.2   FIG. XVII.3

Material: Anthurium blossoms. Caladium and nephthytis foliage.
Form: Triangle.
Line: Crescent.
Color harmony: Monochromatic flowers and contrasting foliage.
Texture: Heavy waxy blossoms, pebbly spadix, smooth foliage.
Finishing: Satin ribbon.
Technique:

This striking corsage of pink, deep rose, and dark crimson anthuriums is definitely modern. Cut the stems of the flowers to 1 inch.

122

PLATE XVII

Triangle of Anthurium Blossoms with Caladium and Nephthytis Foliage

Insert a short, heavy wire up through the stem, stopping just below the base of the flower. Tape the stem to protect and to keep airtight (Fig. XVII.1). Wire over the taped stem with an 18-inch length of 24-gauge wire several times and straighten wire ends. Tape the delicate leaf stems before wiring. Pierce leaves with a hairpin wire just above the base (Fig. XVII.2). Cover all stems completely with green floral tape.

Begin the design with the pointed leaves at the top. The full leaves serve as a foil for the color and also help to support the weight of the luxurious blossoms. Give the light soft pink flower the top spot, with the rose and crimson blossoms swelling out the triangular base.

Curve three stems to complete the crescent line begun by the leaf buds. This crescent within the bold triangular form expresses mastery of designing (Fig. XVII.3).

Tie loops of heavy, rich two-toned satin ribbon to the corsage to emphasize by contrast the exquisitely veined patent leather surface of the anthuriums.

Corsage by: Mrs. William Gray Power.

PLATE XVIII

FIG. XVIII.1   FIG. XVIII.2   FIG. XVIII.3

Material: Yellow waterlily, seagrape foliage.

Form: Circular.

Line: Repeated circles.

Texture: Waxy, glossy, shiny.

Color Harmony: Yellow, yellow/green, bronze.

Finishing: Ribbon-covered wire shaped to repeat the circular movement of flower. Bow of similar color.

Technique:

Drip yellow candle wax or warm paraffin down into the base of the petals around each row.

The waterlily being a little heavier than most flowers is crisscrossed with wires to handle easily. Pierce through the stem at right angles forming an x with two 24-gauge wires, holding parallel to the lower petals. Use more wires if needed. Pull down all wires. Use one to twist around the stem (Fig. XVIII.1). Stretch yellow tape tightly about the stem, starting up under the flower.

The new small round leaves of the seagrape were chosen because of their similarity to the waterlily foliage. The color, too, is a striking foil for the light flower, setting it off majestically. Wire leaves with hairpin wire, twist about stem and tape with yellow tape (Fig. XVIII.2). Choose or cut to size any round leaf in your garden.

The decorative note of the satin-covered wire is easy to master. Tape two 24-gauge or three 26-gauge wires of the 18-inch lengths to supply a good base for the ribbon so it won't slip. Place a knot near

126

PLATE XVIII

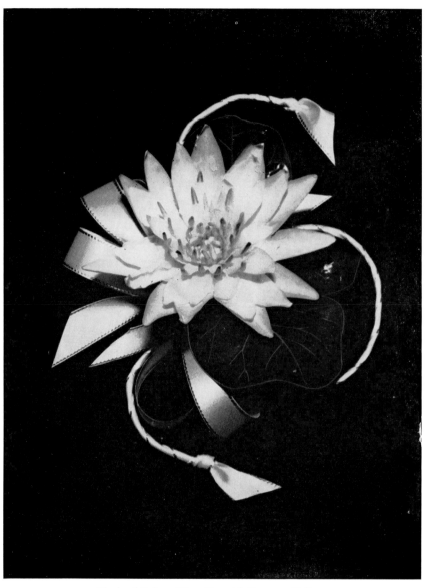

Circle of Yellow Waterlily with Seagrape Foliage

one end, twirl the ribbon down evenly to the lower end. Tie a knot near the second end. Press the wires tightly into back of knots and cut off surplus wire. Cut ribbon tips on slant.

Hold the flower in your hand, arrange three leaves back of the flower, use a double circle of tape to secure. (Fig. XVIII.3). Cut all wire stems short. Make a circle of the ribbon wire beneath the center leaves and curve the two ends to draw the eye back to the center. Attach the ribbon circle and chartreuse bow at left. Position loops so they will appear balanced and well spaced.

Choose any interesting round flower and foliage from your garden to incorporate into this background instead of the waterlily.

Corsage by: Glad Reusch.

PLATE XIX

Fig. XIX.1   Fig. XIX.2   Fig. XIX.3   Fig. XIX.4

Material: Chrysanthemums, pyracantha berries, variegated pothos leaf.
Form: Crescent.
Line: Curved.
Color harmony: Analogous. Orange, red, bronze.
Texture: Pebbly, smooth, dull, tissue.
Finishing: Talisman satin ribbon frame and bow.
Technique:

The Talisman colors of orange through red are carried out in this curved design to be pinned on a circular neckline or to be worn on

PLATE XIX

Crescent of Chrysanthemums, Pyracantha Berries, and Variegated Pothos the shoulder, adjusting curve to fit about the neck. The green accent of the narrow pyracantha leaves and the single pothos leaf at bottom, add to the pleasing silhouette of design.

The orange-bronze chrysanthemums are excellent keepers. Wire by running a short 26-gauge wire into the chrysanthemum. Hook at top and pull down into the blossom. Follow with clutch wiring about the shortened natural-and-wire stem (Fig. XIX.1). Tape.

Small clusters of berries are wired by the clutch method. Start the 26-gauge wire up into the berry cluster and twist about the main stem (Fig. XIX.2). Tape.

Wire the pothos leaf halfway up the blade with a 28-gauge wire hairpin so leaf can be curved gently (Fig. XIX.3). Twist about stem and tape. Cut leaf to size if needed.

The satin-covered frame or platform is made with the regular 18-inch length, 24-gauge wire. Use two wires to give stability. Cover with tape, then with ribbon. The narrow No.2 Talisman ribbon is used for the frame and the bow. Knot ribbon near end of wire. Twist ribbon uniformly down the stem by twirling. Knot near lower end. Press ends of wire down over knots at back of knot. Cut wires short. Form a circle in the center and curve the two ends gently.

Assemble by placing a small group of berries at the left, then at the right. Bind at center with 30-gauge fine wire. Follow alternately, increasing the size toward the center, until all the elements are bound. Place the bottom single leaf and curve gently. Cover assembling wire with a narrow piece of tape (Fig. XIX.4). Fashion a bow of the narrow No.2 Talisman two-toned ribbon. Nestle bow up into design so it won't be too conspicuous. Cut off all surplus wires at back and press tips inward into corsage.

Corsage by: Glad Reusch.

PLATE XX

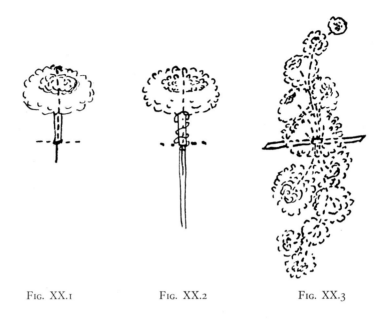

FIG. XX.1   FIG. XX.2   FIG. XX.3

Material: Chrysanthemums.

Form: Double triangle; two-way corsage.

Line: Mild Hogarth.

Color Harmony: Monochromatic.

Texture: Fine, pebbly, smooth, glossy.

Finishing: Fuchsia satin bow, silver stripe on edge to add appeal.

Technique:

The harmony of the deep color in the center of the chrysanthemum matched with the ribbon bow is the dominant color interest. One type of flower can be interesting if the design is eye-catching. Cut all chrysanthemum stems to 1 inch in length. Use 28-gauge wire. Cut short guide wires about 2 inches in length. Pierce this wire up into the blossom from back (Fig. XX.1). Hook wire at top if blossom has very thin stem. Short 9-inch wires are used to bind about the natural-and-wire stem, clutch-fashion (Fig. XX.2). Tape with orchid tape.

The two-way corsage is constructed by starting with the tip bud and building broader toward the base of each triangle. Attach the

PLATE XX

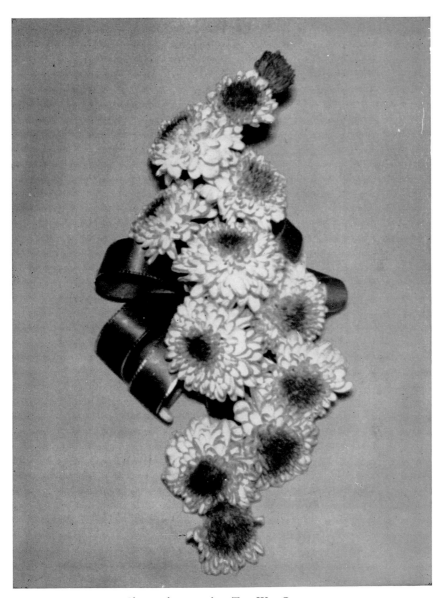

Chrysanthemums in a Two-Way Corsage

first three blossoms one to the other with tape. Repeat for the opposite side and tape together at center. Alternate the placing of remaining chrysanthemums from side to side broadening the triangles as you reach the center. Tape or wire securely. Cover assembly wire if used. Cut surplus stem wires on both sides (Fig. XX.3). Adjust blossoms to form a slight Hogarth curve. Curves are usually more attractive than straight lines.

The bow of fuchsia satin ribbon with silver edge is sized to fit comfortably through the center where the two triangles come together. Any small, round or tubular flower is adaptable to this two-way design. Even florets taken from the snapdragon, tuberose, hyacinth, narcissus, allium, or lycoris are light and airy in the two-way form.

Corsage by: Glad Reusch.

XIII

THE CORSAGE SHOW

A classification for corsages has become a part of almost every flower show, and attracts much attention from visitors. Since beautiful designs can be made with almost any flower, this classification is equally appropriate for specialized shows of roses, tulips, orchids, or iris, as well as seasonal shows of wider range.

Whether the show is a special one for corsages only or is a part of a complete flower show, the exhibitor and the schedule, staging and judging chairmen will have a keen interest in this chapter. An all-corsage show put on at a club, district or state meeting, or at a fair affords an excellent opportunity for skill in judging corsages.

A custom of the day in flower shows is the theme. Such subjects as history of the area, geographical highlights, flags of the country, the state flower, and seasonal connotations are among the themes chosen. In a corsage show, a hat parade, a musical theme, or a jewelry lane would conjure up some interesting classifications.

The Exhibitor

The exhibitor may never want to judge corsages at a show. But if she is apprized of what the judges are expecting in a well-designed corsage and of the perfection they are looking for in technique and workmanship, she will be well on the way to being an outstanding corsage designer. These standards apply whether she fashions flowers for her own pleasure, for the joy of presenting a gift of fine workmanship or of capturing a blue ribbon. If she is cognizant of the requirements set up in the scale of points for judging corsages, she should be able to create exquisite flower accessories.

An exhibitor has certain responsibilities if she is to fulfill all the requirements of the schedule. Read the rules carefully, select the classifications that fit your purpose, and then adhere to every aspect of them by studying the classes you plan to enter. Only well-grown flowers should find their way into a corsage. They should be conditioned thoroughly and, for a show, it is best to put a little moist cotton about each stem before wiring and taping to insure the freshness demanded throughout the length of the show. The corsage exhibit should be kept in show condition by replacing flowers, daily if necessary.

Design a practice corsage a few days in advance of the show, place it against a background and give it a personal appraisal. Turn it over and decide where you can improve your technique. See that the silhouette is pleasing with enough voids to make the design interesting. Check the bow. Be sure it is not too large and that the loops are full and not pressed flat. Fit the loops into the corsage at the focal point so they become a part of the corsage. Be self-expressive and work for wearability as you create a charming accessory to wear every time you attend a club meeting or social affair. The practice designs will improve your technique at show time.

The Schedule Committee

The schedule committee should estimate the ability of the club members when selecting the corsage classes for a show. If the members are novices in corsage craft, the classes should be general, such as "Tailored" and "Evening," or "Informal" and "Formal."

Usually we think of the informal tailored design as one appropriate for daytime wear when a single blossom or a medium-sized spray or foliage is in order. The use of ribbon does not necessarily indicate that a corsage is not in this class. However, ribbon for daytime wear, as mentioned previously, should be consistent with the costume in width and texture, whereas the formal or evening design may go all out in the use of ribbon or accessory material, within the limits of good taste. The formal or evening design is generally styled for formal occasions.

If, however, the club has sponsored numerous corsage workshops, demonstrations, and lectures, the schedule may be more advanced. The theme might be "The Dance," with classes for wristlet, necklace, hair, and bouquet designs. Another theme is "The Club Woman," and the classes feature designs for luncheon and tea, for the president or the guest speaker. A classification for "The Debutante," allows for a great variety of party-going designs, and "The Wedding" for corsages and bouquets for the participants. An "Off the Shoulder" theme might include hat, muff, glove, and purse designs. An all-inclusive theme has classes for the child, sub-deb, debutante, bride, club woman, and grandmother.

A hat parade, where members are adept at this art, with hats made of fresh or dried materials, or with just a trim, wins praise from the audience. A class for the petite with corsages up to 5 inches and a class for the tall girl, matron, or "sophisticate" with corsages up to 8 or 10 inches emphasizes appropriateness in size.

Refer to the heading under "Staging" for inspiration in outlining classes to carry out the theme or title of the class. Be specific in wording. State whether fresh material, dried material, fruit, or foliage is limited.

If the standard scale of points for corsages as below is to be changed, include your special scale of points in the schedule.

Where clubs in an area are studying corsage designing and the corsage exhibit is to be an outstanding part of the flower show, the chairman and her committee may arrange for a Special Corsage Award of Merit.

Staging

Corsages offer a wonderful opportunity to bring beauty into the show. They act as a magnet to draw visitors to the exhibit that stresses ideas for personal grooming and a feeling of being well and appropriately dressed. The staging chairman can plan a most dramatic presentation as she stages a modern, classic, or architecturally sculptured look. Corsages are the jeweled accessories of the show.

The chairman of staging and placing will facilitate judging if she allows corsages to be easily available for judging and places them artistically in the exhibit after judging is completed. The clerk or judge can then handle the corsages, unless specifically stated otherwise in the rules. Each class should be separated by tape, to be removed later. Cellophane bags are frowned upon by many flower-show instructors and judges because the beauty is lost, and the over-all picture is somewhat distorted.

If there is room in the show, a 10-minute demonstration of corsage technique and designing, at intervals, fulfills the responsibility of the show for education. Junior gardeners demonstrating simple corsage techniques always amaze onlookers.

Corsages should be attractively displayed at the flower show. Because individual corsages are small, the staging committee should allow room to accommodate the crowds which gather around an exhibit, even though entries occupy a small amount of space.

Background is an important part of staging, and should be in harmony with the theme of the show. When classifications are also in line with the show theme, an exhibit will be more effective. Care should be taken that the background is not so intricate that it detracts from the corsages.

The height at which the corsages are placed is important. If they can be at eye level, they are effective. Also, the background should be more nearly vertical than horizontal, for corsages are designed to be worn against a vertical surface and the design is lost if looked down upon.

Good lighting or a spotlight over the corsage section is desirable. Show visitors should be able to see but not touch the corsages.

SUGGESTIONS FOR STAGING

The Art Gallery. Where cutouts are made, the corsages are placed to represent the picture. A second board is placed in back on which to pin corsages.

Screens of bamboo, matchsticks, or plain materials.

Wide bands suspended from the roof of the niche or ceiling.

A corsage mobile, or perhaps one for each class.

Three huge rings of Styrofoam on easels or hung from ceiling.

Turn tables in two or more tiers.

A huge color wheel of six segments placed against wall or on easel.
Miniature niches like those used for miniature arrangements.

Fans of natural or tinted bamboo. Actual silk or paper fans, or fans shaped from Celotex or board, and painted.

Boxes, benches, and shelves help in the background set-up. Corrugated paper, about 12 inches in width, curved in and out so one corsage may be placed in each curve. Three heights of these accommodate a large exhibit.

Several large palettes covered with velvet or other material.

A number of large picture frames, one for each class.

If hats are a part of the exhibit, borrow hat stands from a department store. Festoon net from stands to make an enriched background for evening corsages.

Hat boxes, covered with different colored papers for each class, or sprayed with color, offer lids as desirable placements. Tilt boxes to show corsages at correct angle.

A musical scale. Corsages are the notes.

A tree, either made of bare branches—painted, gilded, or coppered—or of fresh pine branches simulating a tree. Try a Christmas-red corsage class on a pine tree.

JUDGING

The chairman of the judges in selecting the panel of three who are to judge corsages might well include, in addition to the two accredited flower-show judges, a third judge whose specialty is corsage designing or who has studied this art.

After the final instructions from the chairman of the judges, the panel will approach the corsage exhibit. The clerk can be especially helpful if she knows the location and number of entries in each class. The judges will note how large the class is and make a rough scaling of the corsages. It is ideal if corsages can be judged at the height at which they are worn. Those that are of poor design or that do not conform to the schedule will be quickly eliminated. The corsage nearest perfection for its class gets the award. Corsages are not judged against each other. Unless there is a close decision, point scoring is not usually done. Corsage designing like flower arranging is the art of organizing the flowers, foliage, ribbons, and other accessories so that they will attain a certain harmony, simplicity, and expression of beauty. Does it give you pleasure? is the final criterion.

The Scales of Points given here are those found on page 142 of the HANDBOOK FOR FLOWER SHOWS of the National Council of State Garden Clubs, Inc. These are also used by all judges accredited by the National Corsage Club, unless the schedule indicates a different scale of points because of theme or other considerations.

Corsages—Fresh Plant Material (Schedule must specify occasion and whether background is provided.)

Technique	15
Design	25
Color	15
Suitable combination of material	15
Distinction	20
Condition	10
	100

Corsages—Dried Material (Schedule must specify occasion and whether background is provided.)

Technique	10
Design	30
Color	10
Combination of materials	20
Originality	15
Distinction	15
	100

Nosegays

Perfection of arrangement	30
Color	25
Distinction and originality	30
Fragrance	15
	100

Note: For dried material comment see page 106 of Handbook.

For nosegay comment see page 108 of Handbook.

The six major considerations listed above in judging fresh flowers are now discussed individually.

Technique

If the judge is able to see the back of the corsage or if the clerk has been advised that she may handle it for the judges' inspection, then it is possible for all 15 points of the scale to be granted, provided the work is excellent. If, however, there is exposed wire, the tape is not stretched so it appears skintight, or if the ends of the stems have not been carefully trimmed and the tape pulled over them, then 1 to 5 points might be deducted. Further deductions might be made if the corsage is poorly assembled, or if it is not firm and upstanding. Should the show chairman indicate that corsages are not to be touched, then the technique points might drop down to 10 or 5 points as the judge could not note the skill or lack of it. The back of the corsage should present a balanced skeleton form, neat, airy, with all lines leading to the focal point. Are stem ends visible? Do they add or detract from the beauty of the design? Does a curved or straight line of stems assure balance and follow the line of the design? In Plate XVII, the wires curve easily in the crescent design to complement the pointed leaf buds at top. In Plate X, the straight wires cut on a slant give stability to the triangular design. The artistry of the corsages shown in Plates I and XV would be ruined if any wire stems were exposed. If the skeleton is good, the outer expression of beauty will speak for itself.

Design

Since the greatest number of points, 25, is given to design, in the fresh flower corsage, the judge should be familiar with the elements and principles of design, especially as they pertain to corsage judging. A corsage is a mobile flower arrangement. It must include the sought-after qualities of line, form, pattern, texture, and color as they apply to wearability. The eye must be led easily into the focal point as it moves from tip to tip in the outer periphery due to a basically good skeleton. The eye then follows the lines into the area of the center of interest.

This solidity at the focal point in turn spreads out to the silhouette by gradation of material or color or through delicacy of form. Well-placed voids of varying shapes add materially to the silhouette of the design.

The principles of design include balance, dominance, contrast, rhythm, proportion, and scale. Here the judge makes a critical study much as a judge proceeds in an art exhibit at a museum. Dividing the number of points allotted into separate amounts for the divisions above, helps in the final judgment of whether 25, 23, or fewer points are the correct estimate. Consideration of the character and style of the corsage design, the artistic value achieved, the over-all quality of the picture created helps in the final decision.

Color

Color, the most dramatic and exultant part of a corsage, becomes very important in corsage judging because of the close harmony required with the background. Fifteen points are allowed in the scale of points, and it must be remembered that the same principles that apply to design above are considered here as they apply to color. In a corsage, a good proportion of color *amounts* used is one (least), two (medium), and three (high). One would represent the brilliant color. Color value diminishes in intensity from the center of interest outward. Look for a pleasing contrast, a coordination of color and design, and a rhythmic flow throughout the corsage. (See Chapter 1 on color harmonies.)

Suitable Combination of Materials

The over-all picture in suitable combination of materials refers not only to the assembled plant materials but their harmony with the background, the ribbon, or other accessory. The interrelationship of all buds, flowers, and foliage, particularly when a number of different flowers are used, is of utmost importance. Too many extraneous types reduce the chance of suitability.

Distinction

Distinction. The word suggests what we hope we have accomplished in our corsage design. The 20 points allotted are for marked superiority, the manner in which the design is executed. This is where the superb craftsman can show her skill in mechanical technique and artistic expression, and come up with a refreshing and inspiring idea in her corsage because of the way she has handled her material.

Condition

The last 10 points to consider are for condition of the plant material in a corsage, the perkiness of the bow, not one that shows former tying or is mussed in any way. The blooms must possess substance, freshness, and turgidity. There should be no sign of limpness, blemishes, or evidence of disease, but the judge need not be so aware of cultural perfection as she is when judging a horticultural specimen.

The judge is now ready to add up the points she deducted from each of the headings in the scale and see how near the corsage comes to a blue ribbon. If in her cursory judging she considered the exhibit worthy of a blue ribbon and it now falls short, she may want to re-evaluate, particularly if the other two judges list it for a blue ribbon. Perhaps they can point to a determining feature and all judges see eye to eye. Wise and prudent decisions come from experience in judging as well as a thorough understanding of the art involved.

THE CORSAGE FASHION SHOW

The corsage fashion show is a new type of garden club entertainment and education. The show may feature corsages modeled by the designers, or may be in cooperation with a dress shop, the clothes worn by professional models, the corsages made by club members. The commentator should remark on the flowers as well as the styles.

The fashion show of wide range might begin with clothes and flowers suitable for children and proceed for the teen age, the debutante, the club member, and honor guest. A more elaborate show might even include costumes for afternoon, dinner, and dancing.

A light note might be planned around a Tom Thumb wedding, with children taking the parts and flower designs scaled down to size. This is good experience for the club members, as miniature corsage designs are just as important as larger forms and are fascinating to make.

If time permits, the style show might be preceded with a showing of kodachrome slides of corsages, or a demonstration of technique. The corsage fashion show might be a special feature presented during the flower show.

PLATE XXI

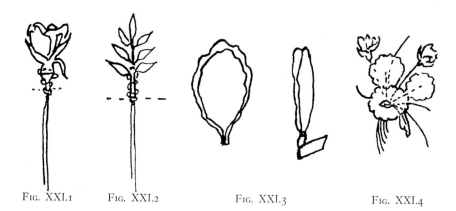

Material: Tiny Cecil Brunner roses, foliage and flowers of orange
    jessamine (*Murraea exotica*), rolled petals of pink Radiance rose.

Form: Circle.

Line: Semi-circle.

Color Harmony: Pink, rose, green, white.

Texture: Smooth, rough, tissue.

Finishing: Silver wire braid, green stems, silver/pink bow.

Technique:

    This petite corsage planned for the sub-teenager measures only
$3\frac{1}{2}$ x 4 inches. The smallest type plant material is chosen to keep
the entire corsage in good scale and appropriate to the age. The roses,
Cecil Brunner, are wired by the piercing method, 28-gauge wire,
inserted through the green calyx (Fig. XXI.1). Tape.

    The tip ends of foliage of the orange jessamine with its fragrant,
delicate white blossoms left on the natural stems, are wired about the
base of stem, clutch method, by merely wrapping around a few times
and straightening the wires for stem (Fig. XXI.2). Tape.

    Two medium-colored rose petals are placed one on top of the
other and rolled for bud. Tape end to protect and wire by the clutch
method with 28-gauge wire (Fig. XXI.3). This deeper color accent
adds interest at the focal point near bottom.

    Assemble by holding the small flowers in the hand beginning at
the top and placing one by one, first the rosebud to left, then the top
foliage, the rosebud to right, and work toward the center with the

PLATE XXI

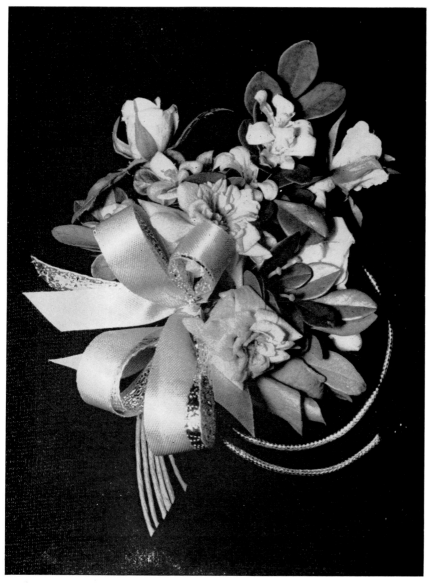

Semi-Circle of Cecil Brunner Roses, Orange Jessamine, and Rolled Petals of
Radiance Rose

foliage and opened roses. The rolled rosebud is placed at bottom for deeper color accent (Fig. XXI.4).

A 9-inch length of silver braid circled for a background, with carefully placed curved end, completes the design along with a small bow of narrow No. 2 pink satin and silver ribbon. Place one length on top of the other and tie bow with very short loops.

Experiment with other tiny material from your garden, keeping within the confines of the 3- to 5-inch corsage.

Corsage by: Glad Reusch.

PLATE XXII

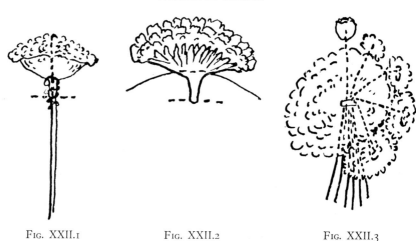

FIG. XXII.1   FIG. XXII.2   FIG. XXII.3

Material: Aster, button chrysanthemums.
Form: Circular.
Line: Circular swirl.
Color Harmony: Analogous.
Texture: Fine, pebbly, soft, with contrasting smooth, satiny.
Finishing: Narrow double-faced ribbon, orchid with fuchsia picot.
Technique:

The simplicity of the easy movement in this aster and chrysanthemum corsage as the smaller flowers circle about the aster in the center spells charm and wearability. Cut stems of flowers short, use the hook method and the clutch wiring for the small chrysanthemums. 28-gauge wire is correct for the small flowers (Fig. XXII.1). The large aster requires a heavier wire, 24-gauge. Remove surplus

148

PLATE XXII

Swirl of Aster and Button Chrysanthemums

green at base of flower. Pierce through the green calyx from side to side (Fig. XXII.2). Pull the wires down and twist one around the other down the short stem. Straighten wires. Tape.

Assemble by starting with the aster. Place the small button chrysanthemums about the aster. The graceful gradation of flowers from the top bud down to the full bloom of the small chrysanthemum follows a desirable art principle. Stems are spread evenly at the base of the corsage and cut to follow the curved line. About one-third of the length of the entire corsage is a good measurement for the wires (Fig. XXII.3). In some designs it will be less than this, and in others no stems at all will be exposed. Avoid stems that are too long. Each group of stems should be considered as it completes the balance of the entire corsage.

The charm of this bow is in the width and fullness. No. 2, the narrow ribbon, in complimentary orchid color with a fuchsia picoted edge, completes the circular movement of aster, swirl, and circled loops of ribbon.

Corsage by: Glad Reusch.

PLATE XXIII

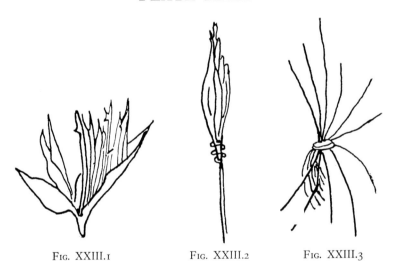

| Fig. XXIII.1 | Fig. XXIII.2 | Fig. XXIII.3 |

Material: Bird of paradise (*Strelitzia reginae*).
Form: Half circle.
Line: Swirling half wheel or semi-circular.

150

PLATE XXIII

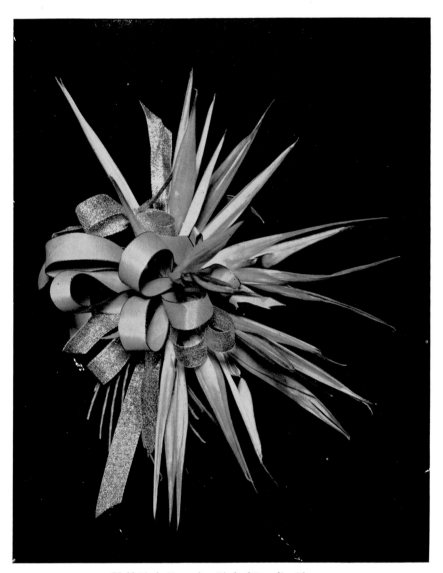

Half Circle Featuring Bird of Paradise Flower

Color Harmony: Blue, orange, yellow.

Texture: Smooth, linear, pebbly, dull.

Finishing: Gold bows with yellow taffeta ribbon.

Technique:

From the rather heavy pod of the bird of paradise come the striking segments of orange-yellow petals and blue spears. It is indeed an exotic looking corsage when the designer makes use of all of the pointed florets and rearranges them into a modern formal expression of art.

Separate the florets by slipping the fingers into the pod very gently and pulling out one group at a time. Discard the pod (Fig. XXIII.1).

Reduce the base of the floret if too heavy or bulky. Wire each floret with a 26-gauge wire, piercing it through in upper third of base (Fig. XXIII.2). Twist wire about stem, and cover with yellow tape.

Form into a semi-circle using the blue beaks for accent (Fig. XXIII.3). Arrange stems into a pleasing curve. If stems are too numerous cut some off short under the focal point.

Try a wristlet or hair arrangement. A few may be arranged to simulate a bird in flight.

Corsage by: Mrs. Ray O. Edwards.

PLATE XXIV

FIG. XXIV.1   FIG. XXIV.2   FIG. XXIV.3   FIG. XXIV.4

Material: Amaryllis, begonia, rose.

Form: Circular.

Line: Color line dominant, semi-circular.

Color Harmony: Monochromatic—pink through rose.

Texture: Waxy, velvety, shiny silver-edged ribbon.

Finishing: Half of stems removed. Remaining half covered with silver-edged ribbon and curved slightly to round out design. Bow of same deep rose satin ribbon.

Technique:

A swirl of amaryllis petals sets the key for the design. Separate petals from amaryllis keeping as much of lower end as possible. Place a tiny bit of cotton, moistened, about the base. Push a 28-gauge narrow hairpin wire through petal near base, vertically, and twist one wire about the stem and other wire, clutch method, to the end of stem, and straighten wires (Fig. XXIV.1). Tape.

The begonia blossoms, separated into small groups, are wired by the clutch method with 28-gauge wire. Allow the wire to catch up into the lowest flower stem. Twist wire a few times, straighten, and tape (Fig. XXIV.2).

154

PLATE XXIV

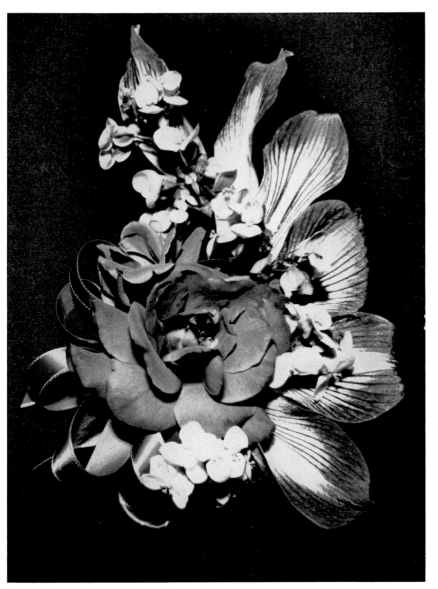

Swirl of Amaryllis, Begonia, and Rose

The piercing method is used for the rose. Pierce through the green calyx with a heavy 24-gauge wire. Pull wires down, twist a few times, and tape stem (Fig. XXIV.3). Repeat on rose bud.

Assemble the corsage by starting with the wired amaryllis swirl. Position the petals uniformly and bind at focal point (Fig. XXIV.4).

Handle the begonia groups by starting with the top one and attaching the remaining groups one to the other for the entire right hand movement inside the amaryllis petals. The lower groups are turned back on themselves and bound at focal point after roses are placed.

Attach the rose and bud at base so they will nestle into this glamorous amaryllis flare. This is a daring conception of a modern, exotic combination. Use any lily petal and other flower combinations to create a similar effect. For a small person, use about half the material and proportion the corsage with smaller lily petals and roses.
Corsage by: Glad Reusch.

PLATE XXV

| Fig. XXV.1 | Fig. XXV.2 | Fig. XXV.3 | Fig. XXV.4 |

Material: Miniature and medium yellow daylilies, lavender solanum.
Form: Triangle.
Line: Circular repetition of flowers with accent points at top.

PLATE XXV

Triangle of Yellow Daylilies and Lavender Solanum

Color Harmony: Complementary.

Texture: Fine, crinkly, ribbed, smooth, shiny.

Finishing: Yellow-taped stems, yellow satin bow.

Technique:

The complementary colors of yellow and lavender lend a pastel harmony to this corsage. The miniature daylilies, slightly darker in value, offer an easy gradation in size up to the buds and delicate lavender-colored solanum clusters, which vary from bud form to full bloom.

Wire the small daylilies and buds with the clutch method, 28-gauge fine wire (Fig. XXV.1), and the large daylily with the piercing method so the daylily can be faced out easily without breaking the stem (Fig. XXV.2). Yellow tape carries out the harmony.

The lavender solanum clusters are wired with 28-gauge wire. Start the wire up into the cluster, twist around short stem, straighten wires and tape (Fig. XXV.3).

Assemble the corsage by starting with the top buds and solanum. Bind these three stems together with a small strip of tape. Add the miniature blossoms, and bind with tape at focal point under the large blossom. Insert the remaining clusters at each side. Position the yellow daylily at center and turn the lower blossoms back on themselves to create depth. Bind securely at focal point with yellow tape (Fig. XXV.4). Tape is often preferred to fine wire for assembling where corsage is light. Shorten unwanted stems in back near center. Add a small yellow bow, just large enough to present a slight shiny variation in the texture and complete the design. Balance design by retaining only those stems that will complete the picture.

When daylilies are out of season choose from among these flowers for a similar design—daffodil, hollyhock, peony, rose, tigridia, tulip (opened), tulip tree, or any lily form in your garden.

Corsage by: Glad Reusch.

PLATE XXVI

Material: Frangipani (*Plumeria*), chrysanthemums, eucalyptus foliage.
Form: Crescent intertwined Hogarth curve.
Line: Color line, strong contrast.
Color Harmony: Complementary contrast.
Texture: Velvety, smooth, fine.
Finishing: Satin rope loops.
Technique:

This modern corsage of strong contrast with white chrysanthemums and dubonnet frangipani, has still another note of interest in the complementary green of foliage and satin loops. It is bold, wearable, and striking. Reduce the size for the small figure.

Wire the white chrysanthemums by first placing a hooked wire through the center of blossom, then follow with clutch wiring around the short stem end of hook wire (Fig. XXVI.1). Tape with green tape.

The frangipani is the favorite fragrant blossom used extensively for leis in the Hawaiian Islands. It grows abundantly out-of-doors in the Deep South. Place a wisp of cotton about the tender stem.

PLATE XXVI

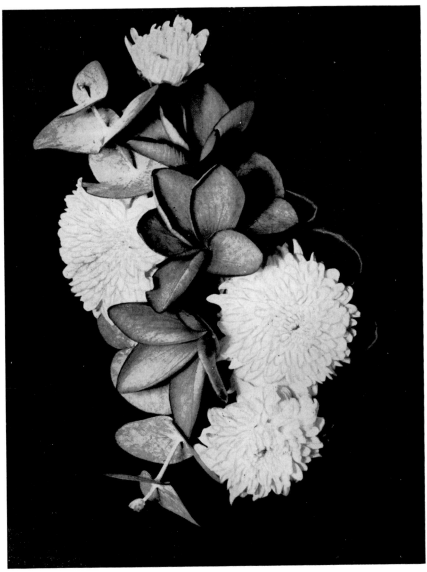

Modified Crescent of Frangipani, Chrysanthemums, and Eucalyptus Foliage

Wire around the cotton, clutch method, with a 28-gauge fine wire (Fig. XXVI.2).

Cut the eucalyptus silvery green foliage into desirable lengths. Wire, 26-gauge, with the clutch method around the stem (Fig. XXVI.3).

Assemble by starting with the chrysanthemum bud at top, then add foliage, the two dark frangipani and the top chrysanthemum. Arrange lower half by starting with eucalyptus tip, two chrysanthemums, and the frangipani. Wire the two component parts together and cut off surplus wires (Fig. XXVI.4). Cover the assembling wire with tape.

To emphasize the modern color line, no bow is used. Instead, remove the wire from the green satin tubing, make three loops, wire and tape, and attach at right. Substitute any round blossom from your garden. Many spring bulb flowers could substitute for the frangipani. Yellow-and-white color schemes are particularly attractive after a season without bloom.

Corsage by: Glad Reusch.

APPENDIX

CHART I—CORSAGE FLOWERS

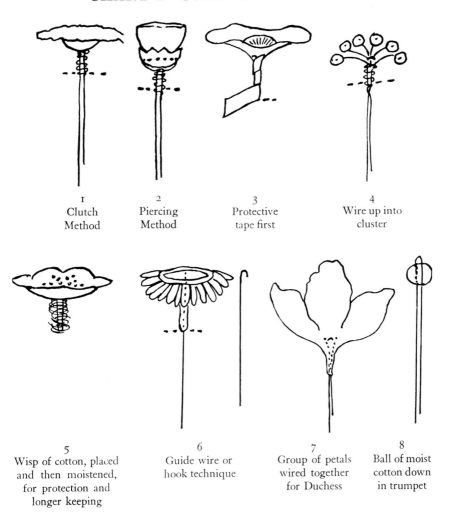

1
Clutch
Method

2
Piercing
Method

3
Protective
tape first

4
Wire up into
cluster

5
Wisp of cotton, placed
and then moistened,
for protection and
longer keeping

6
Guide wire or
hook technique

7
Group of petals
wired together
for Duchess

8
Ball of moist
cotton down
in trumpet

Note: Wiring techniques are indicated by numbers which refer to the sketches above. In some instances, certain varieties of a given flower require different techniques, but those given here are the most frequently used.

Durability for the given number of days depends upon proper conditioning of the flowers as indicated in Chapter III. Special treatment for certain flowers is noted under Suggestions and Comments.

Flower	*Wiring*	*Days of Durability*	*Suggestions and Comments*
Abutilon (Flowering maple)	5 & 2	3	Bell-shaped flowers. Handle carefully.
Acacia	1	10	Delightful, spray-like yellow. Use for accent with yellow-centered flowers.
African daisy	6 & 1	6	Dainty.
Agapanthus (Lily of the Nile)	4	3	Cut stem very short. Fragrant blue bells in umbels.
Ageratum	4 & 5	2	Everblooming. Colonial type.
Allamanda	7, 3 & 2	1	Clear yellow trumpet. Fleeting. See Plate V.
Allium cepa	4	5	Dainty white with black center. Slight onion odor.
Althaea	2	2	Substitute for hibiscus.
Alstroemeria	8	4	Wire each flower individually. Extraordinary color range.
Alyssum	4	1	Excellent for outer circle of colonial. Plunge completely in cold water.
Amaryllis	7	3	Remove pollen. Use petals for Duchess form.
Amazon lily	8	4	See EUCHARIS GRANDIFLORA.
Andromeda	4	4	A graceful drooping pendant.
Anemone	6 & 1	5	Accent center color with matching ribbon.
Anthemis tinctoria (Golden Camomile)	6 & 1	4	Yellow and new shades.
Anthurium	3 & 1	10	Exotic patent leather flowers for modern designs.
Aster	6 & 1 or 2	3	Remove part of green calyx to lighten.
Armeria	4 or 1	10	See STATICE.
Astilbe	1	3	Use soft, fluffy tips to point design.
Azalea	8, 2 & 1	3	Pick only buds and flowers needed, saving wood stock. Put stem in ½ tsp. oil of peppermint for few minutes.

CHART I   165

Flower	Wiring	Days of Durability	Suggestions and Comments
Babysbreath	4	4	Annual variety larger flower and more durable.
Begonia, tuberous	Special	3	Wire like Camellia. See Chapter IV.
Beloperone guttata	4	6	See SHRIMP PLANT.
Bird-of-Paradise-Flower (Strelitzia reginae)	1	10	Slit big pod carefully and lift petals out. Separate and wire in small groups.
Bouvardia	5 & 4	4	Lay moist cotton over flowers in box.
Bridal wreath	4	2	See SPIRAEA.
Calendula	6 & 1	5	Scald lower stem. Accent brown centers with brown grasses and seeds.
Calla	3 & 1	4	Miniature white is excellent corsage size. Paint spadix with clear nail polish. Tie stem with thread to avoid splitting.
Calycanthus floridus (Sweetshrub)	2	6	An old-time favorite with a fragrant clove scent.
Camellia	Special	4	Wiring instructions Chapter IV. Condition in ¼ tsp. boric acid to 2 qts. water.
Carnation	2	10	Snap stem off. Put in ¼ tsp. boric acid to 2 qts. water. Few drops of water on petals.
Cattail (miniature)	1	10	Will keep indefinitely if painted with shellac or clear nail polish to prevent bursting. Freshen in vinegar solution.
Cattleya	3 & 1	10	Between wearings turn back floral tape and put stem in water.
Chamaelaucium	4	24	See "GERALDTON WAXFLOWER."
Cherry, Oriental flowering	3 & 1	2	Peel bark, cut stem crisscross. Double variety good substitute for tiny roses.
Christmas cactus	3 & 1	4	Grow indoors. Delightful for Christmas designs.
Christmas rose	5 & 1	2	See HELLEBORUS NIGER.
Chrysanthemum	6 & 1	10	Some require #1 wiring only. Feather big blossoms.
Clematis	5 & 1	2	Good form and colors.
Clerodendron	4	10	Dries beautiful dubonnet.

Flower	*Wiring*	*Days of Durability*	*Suggestions and Comments*
Clivia	8	5	Flaming orange clusters. Wire flowers individually.
Clover	3 & 1	3	Use white and red. See Plate III.
Coralbean	3 & 2	3	See ERYTHRINA CRISTA-GALLI.
Coralbells (Heuchera)	4	5	Delicate pointed forms for lightness.
Cornflower	6 & 1	10	White, pink, blue. Excellent corsage material.
Cosmos	3 & 1	1	Light and airy.
Crape myrtle	5 & 1	1	Tissue paper texture. Dainty.
Crocus	8	2	Open wide for variety. Fine spring corsage flower.
Cyclamen	3 & 1	4	Pull from bulb. Cut stem under water and soak.
Cymbidium	3 & 1	14	If fresh when cut, may last 1 month or more.
Cypripedium (Ladyslipper)	3 & 1	10	Slice fraction from stem end daily.
Daffodil	1	3	Pick fresh for long life. Condition in shallow water.
Dahlia	3 & 1	3	Scald stem. Choose from pompon, quill, and shaggy types. For large types wire as for Camellias in Chapter IV.
Daisy	6 & 1	5	1 tsp. peppermint oil to 1 qt. water. Also see SHASTA DAISY.
Daphne	4	3	Fragrant. Use D. cneorum and D. odora.
Daucus carota	4	1	See QUEEN-ANNE'S-LACE.
Daylily (Hemerocallis)	1 or 7	1	If desired for evening, pick bud in morning before it opens and place in refrigerator. Or keep open by inserting a round flower in center.
Delphinium	3 & 1	2	Fine range of blues. Pick individual florets from spike as needed. Teaspoonful of alcohol in water.
Dendrobium	3 & 1	5	Dainty spray orchids. See Plate XVI.
Dianthus	2	4	See PINK.
Dogwood	1	3	Use for smart tailored designs.
Doronicum	6 & 1	4	Early spring daisy form.

CHART I   167

Flower	Wiring	Days of Durability	Suggestions and Comments
Epidendrum	3 & 1	10	Spray orchids. Wire individually. Combine with larger flowers of harmonious colors and textures.
Epiphyllum	3 & 1	5	Use varied forms for exotic designs.
Erythrina crista-galli (Coralbean)	3 & 2	3	Striking warm, bright colors. Called "Cry-baby tree."
Eucharis grandiflora (Amazon lily)	8	4	Very fragile. Handle carefully. Elegant and waxy.
Euphorbia	6 & 1	2	Delightful succulents.
Feverfew	1	10	Button type useful to lighten design and for colonials.
"Flowering maple"	5 & 2	3	See ABUTILON.
Forgetmenot	5 & 1	3	Annual best and largest flower. Others, scald bottom inch of stem for 2 minutes.
Freesia	8	4	Cut through green stem above white portion to harden.
Fuchsia	2	3	Pick separately as needed and place immediately in shallow pan.
Gaillardia	2	5	Excellent color range for summer designs.
Galanthus	4	3	See SNOWDROP.
Gardenia	5 or 3 & 1	3	Keep in airtight box when not in use. Place moist cotton over blossom. Best variety is Mystery.
"Geraldton waxflower" (Chamaelaucium)	4	24	Perfect for dainty spray work.
Geranium	5 & 4	3	Many delightful hybrids provide wide color range. Foliage also desirable, especially after frost.
Gerbera	1 or 2	7	Brilliant colors. Also use double varieties.
Geum	6 & 1	4	Scald stem, then plunge in deep water.
Gladiolus	2 or 7	2	Cut stalk when lowest floret opens. Put in strong vinegar water. Spray petals when not wearing. For Glamellia, see Plate VI.
Gloriosa (Glory lily)	3 & 1	5	Remove pollen. Unusual form. Exotic.
Golden Camomile	6 & 1	4	See ANTHEMIS TINCTORIA.

Flower	Wiring	Days of Durability	Suggestions and Comments
Goldenrod	1	5	Scald stem. Reduce as needed to fit scale of design.
Grape hyacinth	1	4	Excellent for blue accent in spring.
Grand Duke Jasmine	5 & 1	2	See JASMINUM SAMBAC.
Heather	1	10	Use small sprigs with dominant flowers.
Helleborus niger (Christmas rose)	5 & 1	2	Drinks through petals. Submerge completely. Cover corsage with damp cotton.
Helenium	6 & 1	5	Richly colored autumn flowers.
Helichrysum (Strawflower)	6 & 1	10	Everlasting if dried in bud or half-open stage.
Hemerocallis	1 or 7	1	See DAYLILY.
Heuchera	4	5	See CORALBELLS.
Hibiscus	2	1	For night use, place bud in refrigerator before sunup.
Hollyhock	2	2	Scald or scorch stem. New double varieties are excellent for corsages.
Hydrangea	5 & 1	3	Plunge completely, then soak in deep water. Also good as dried material.
Hyacinth	8	5	Squeeze out slippery substance, then put in deep water. Wire individual florets.
Iris	1 or 2	4	Cut in bud. Dutch, Siberian, and Ochroleuca best. Bearded iris very fragile. Wrap in wet paper.
Ixora	4	3	Small clusters, waxy.
Jasminum sambac (Grand Duke Jasmine)	5 & 1	2	Perfect tiny white rose form with superb fragrance. Use for floral jewelry.
Kalmia latifolia (Mountain laurel)	4	3	Fine cluster formation.
Laceflower (Trachymene)	4	3	Fine textured circles of florets. Formerly called Didiscus.
Ladyslipper	3 & 1	10	See CYPRIPEDIUM.
Larkspur	1	3	Dainty spike.
Leucocoryne ixioides	5 & 1	3	Tiny flowers. See Plate VIII.

CHART 1   169

Flower	Wiring	Days of Durability	Suggestions and Comments
Lilac	5 & 1	2	Crush stem. Moist cotton helps keep fresh.
Lily	3 & 1	3	Remove pollen. Use #7 wiring for Duchess form.
Lily of the Nile	4	3	See AGAPANTHUS.
Lily of the valley	1	6	Pull from bulb. Cut stem under water. Soak for 2 hours, then hang upside down in refrigerator to harden.
Liriodendron tulipifera	2	5	See TULIPTREE.
Lotus	5 & 1	3	Pick as buds open.
Lycoris	5 & 4	5	Intricate and delicate flower head.
Magnolia	3 & 1	2	Careful handling. Use M. stellata and M. sieboldi for tailored, and M. soulangeana for evening.
Marguerite	6 & 1	5	Long flowering. Always pert looking.
Marigold	6 & 1	5	Velvety yellow to mahogany. Small ones good. Avoid varieties with strong odor.
Meadowrue	4	5	See THALICTRUM.
Mockorange	3 & 1	3	Fragrant, sweet odor.
Mountain laurel	4	3	See KALMIA LATIFOLIA.
Narcissus	3 & 1	3	Dozens of varieties, all desirable. Cheerfulness double an old-time favorite.
Nerine	3 & 1	5	Spidery flower.
Nicotiana	5 & 1	2	Fragrant, star-like. Scald stem, then cold bath.
Orange blossom	5 & 1	3	Waxy, fragrant.
Orchid	3 & 1, or 6 & 1	10	Many varieties, many long lasting. See CATTLEYA, CYMBIDIUM, CYPRIPEDIUM, DENDROBIUM, EPIDENDRUM, and PHALAENOPSIS.
Ornithogalum (Star-of-Bethlehem)	1	6	Black and white contrast.
Pansy	5 & 1	2	Wire three at once and crowd together. Try a pansy ring.
Pentstemon	8	2	Scald stem. Charming tubelike flowers. Native blue spectacular.
Peony	1	3	Scald stem, then deep water bath. Few drops of water on petals.
Petunia, ruffled	5 & 1	2	1 tsp. sugar to 1 pt. water.

Flower	Wiring	Days of Durability	Suggestions and Comments
Phalaenopsis	3 & 1	2	"Moth orchids" in pink or white. Use one or two in hair design.
Pieris floribunda	1	3	Lacy effect with other flowers.
Pink (Dianthus)	2	4	Fragrant. Good color range.
Poinsettia	5 & 1	1	Flamboyant and bizarre. Dip stem end in boiling water.
Pomegranate	2	3	Flowers and fruit usable.
Poppy	5 & 1	1	Iceland poppy and double varieties best.
Primrose	4	4	P. polyantha and P. auricula very fine varieties. Primroses give some people a rash.
Pyrethrum	6 & 1	6	Excellent daisy form and delightful colors.
Queen-Anne's-lace (Daucus carota)	4	1	Scald stem then cold bath. Good for delicate white touch.
Ranunculus	1	7	Fine color range.
Rhododendron	8	6	Pick separate florets and harden in shallow pan.
Rose	2 or 6 & 1	3	Cut above joint. Burn tip of stem. Use own foliage.
Scabiosa	1	3	Interesting color pickup.
Scilla	4	3	Pull from bulb, then cut stem short. Effective spikes.
Shasta daisy	6 & 1	5	Esther Reed is aristocrat of the white daisies. 1 tsp. peppermint oil to 1 qt. water.
Shrimp plant (Beloperone guttata)	4	6	Queer form, subdued color.
Snapdragon	2	3	Wire individual blooms, spikes are too heavy.
Snowdrop (Galanthus)	4	3	Use #8 if bells are wired individually.
Spathyphyllum	5 & 1	10	Similar to tiny calla lily.
Spiraea (Bridal wreath)	4	2	Use for lightness.

CHART I   171

Flower	Wiring	Days of Durability	Suggestions and Comments
Star-of-Bethlehem	1	6	See ORNITHOGALUM.
Statice (Armeria)	4 or 1	10	Lasts indefinitely if dried.
Stephanotis	8 or 3 & 1	10	Fragrant, waxy, choice bell shape. Favorite for wedding bouquets.
Stock	5 & 1	3	Wire florets individually.
Stokesia	6 & 1	4	Good form.
Strawflower	6 & 1	10	See HELICHRYSUM.
Strelitzia reginae	1	10	See BIRD-OF-PARADISE-FLOWER.
Sweet pea	4	3	Fragile, but desirable.
Sweetshrub	2	6	See CALYCANTHUS FLORIDUS.
Sweet william	4	5	Cluster heads of unusual markings and rich colors.
Thalictrum (Meadowrue)	4	5	Delicate lavender spikes.
Tigridia	3 & 1	1	Fine summer bulb.
Trachymene	4	3	See LACEFLOWER.
Trillium	5 & 1	2	Pick only the flower. Leaves are necessary for next year's bloom.
Trollius	1	5	Globelike. Architectural beauty.
Tuberose	8 or 3 & 1	5	Two tsp. salt to 2 qts. water. Layer of cotton over corsage in box.
Tulip	6 & 1	3	Open wide by carefully pressing petals back one by one. Use for bouquets and muffs.
Tuliptree (Liriodendron tulipifera)	2	5	Rare orange and green combination. Also called yellow poplar. Crush woody stem.
Verbena	4	5	Usable cluster. Brilliant red good for patriotic corsage.
Viburnum	4	3	V. carlesi, V. burkwoodi very fragrant and waxy.
Viola	3 & 1	2	Stagger and wire three at once. Pick frequently, more will come.
Violet	3 & 1	2	Dip flowers in water a few moments. Use in small groups with other flowers, or in bunches with own foliage.
Wallflower	5 & 4	1	Plush velvet, wide color range.

Flower	Wiring	Days of Durability	Suggestions and Comments
Waterlily	6 & 1	3	If picked on first day open, will last 3 days. Otherwise, drop paraffin (warm enough to run) among petals.
Watsonia	8	3	Small pastel trumpets.
Wild flowers, assorted	5 & 1	2	Cut in bud. Take jar of water to field, and plunge buds immediately.
Wistaria	4	2	Scald stem. Good choice for drooping effect.
Yucca	5 & 1	5	Wire florets separately.
Zinnia	6 & 1	4	Scald stem, then deep bath. Miniature and Fantasy excellent for corsages.

CHART II—CORSAGE FOLIAGES

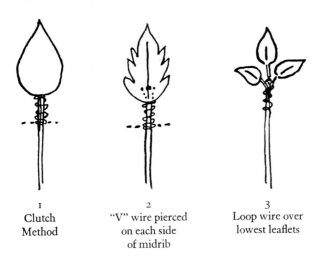

1	2	3
Clutch Method	"V" wire pierced on each side of midrib	Loop wire over lowest leaflets

Note: Wiring instructions refer to the sketches at the top of the page. Certain varieties may require different treatment from the ones indicated below, but these are generally the most satisfactory.

Foliage	Wiring	Suggestions
Abelia	3	Glossy red-bronze tips. Fine texture.
Acacia baileyana	1	Blue-green, lacey.
Aglaonema simplex	2	See Chinese evergreen.
Amaranthus	2	Dark red colors.
Aralia	1	Cut to desired size. White edge effective.
Artemisia silver king	1	Slender gray tips. Long lasting.
Bamboo	1	Condition 1 hour in very salty water.
Banana	2	Use flower petals as foliage. Rich, wine-red. Heavy.
Beet	2	Rich mahogany hues.
Begonia	2	Heavily veined, rich, lustrous. Cut down large leaves.
Berberis darwini (Barberry)	3	Tiny holly-like leaf. Other red leaved barberries useful also.

Foliage	Wiring	Suggestions
Blueberry	1	Keep plants in sun and dry for rich coloring.
Box	3	Uniform sprightly small green leaves.
Broom	1	Use curved tips of the Scotch broom.
Caladium	1 or 2	Rich marking and veining. Cut down if too large.
Calla	2	Yellow-spotted is good. Cut down. Plunge in water.
Camellia	2	Glossy. Excellent keeper.
Carnation	1	Group tufts and curlicues together before wiring. Splendid gray-green color.
Cattail	1	Cut down or loop. Almost everlasting. Good for bronzing or painting.
Cedar	1	Desirable texture.
Chamaecyparis	3	See FALSECYPRESS.
Chinese evergreen (Aglaonema simplex)	2	Heart-shaped green and variegated.
Chrysanthemum	2	Rich texture. Use with own flowers.
Coleus	2	Plunge in water. Wide range of colors.
Cornflower	1	Gray-green. Fine color.
Crocus	1	Use in bundles.
Croton	2	Exotic color. If cut down, use #2 wiring. To avoid stain, paint edge of cut leaf with clear nail polish or thin glue. An alternate is to spray the entire leaf with a plastic foliage spray at a 70-degree room temperature.
Cyclamen	2	Heart-shaped, mottled and veined. Plunge in water.
Daffodil	2	Strap-like, blue-green. Cut down or loop. Substitute foliage for ribbon bow.
Dahlia	2	Use with dahlia blossoms.
Dieffenbachia	1	Smooth, desirable accent.
Dogwood	1	Violet-red tinge is useful.
Dracaena	2	Yellow-green markings are smart.
Eucalyptus	1	Excellent keeper. Slender and dollar-shaped leaves.
Euonymus	3	Vari-colored.
Falsecypress (Chamaecyparis)	3	Extremely fine texture. Use for delicate contrast. Some varieties formerly called Retinospera. "Golden Cypress" has yellow-green foliage fine for corsages.
Fern	1 or 3	Some ferns excellent. Experiment. Maid-

CHART II 175

Foliage	Wiring	Suggestions
		enhair poor keeper. Burn ends. Place between wet newspaper.
Fungus	2	Tree fungus. Leave round or cut to strips.
Funkia	2	See HOSTA.
Galax	2	Woodsy fragrance. Turns bronze. Fine circular form. Use to back corsages.
Gardenia	2	Use old leaves. Plunge several hours.
Geranium	2	Frost colors gloriously. Crinkly, waxy. Rose geranium very fragrant.
Ginkgo	1	Maidenhair shape. Clear yellow color in fall.
Gladiolus	2	Straplike. Long lasting. Make loops for foliage bow.
Hen-and-Chickens	1	Unique form. Durable. Cool appearance for hot weather.
Holly	1	Glossy, pointed.
Hosta (Plantain lily, Funkia)	2	Cream, yellow and white markings. Reduce size.
Huckleberry	3	Lasts for weeks. Sprays of green and bronze.
Hydrangea	2	Rich green.
Iris	2	Cut to size. Strong accent for modern design.
Ivy	2 or 1	Use individual leaves in small designs, sprays for trailing effect in bouquets. Excellent choice for metallic painting.
Japanese Plum	2	See LOQUAT.
Juniper	3	Tiny scaled evergreen. Use in winter designs for contrast with smooth surfaces.
Kale	2	Very decorative. Use when chartreuse and dubonnet needed.
Laurel	1	Broad, glossy. Fine keeper.
Lemon	1	Good substitute for camellia foliage.
Lichen	3	Reindeer moss commonest. Fine color and minute textural note.
Ligustrum	1	Substitute for camellia foliage.
Lily of the valley	1	Chartreuse when grown indoors. Use

Foliage	*Wiring*	*Suggestions*
		with white flowers for contrast against white dress.
Loquat		
(Japanese plum)	2	Cut to size. Heavy veining, woolly, dull texture.
Magnolia grandiflora	2	Cut to size. Dark green fresh. Dries fine brown. Use solution of glycerine and water for antique finish.
Mahonia	2	See Oregon Grape.
Maple	1	Japanese maples best for size and color.
Mistletoe	3	Thick velvety leaves.
Monstera	2	Cut to desired size. Glossy.
Nandina	3	Highly colored tiny leaves. Crush stem and soak in water.
Narcissus	1	Blue-green, straplike.
Nephthytis	1	Heart shape good. See Plate XVII.
Oak	1	Place in half water half glycerine solution to preserve color.
Oregon grape		
(Mahonia)	2	Glossy. Use like holly.
Pachysandra	1	Scalloped, roseate form.
Pandanus		
(Screwpine)	2	Cut to size. Strong, swordlike.
Pelargonium	2	Crinkly, fragrant. Rose perfume. Colors redden with frost.
Peony	2	Fine fall colors.
Peperomia	1	Thick and dull.
Periwinkle		
(Vinca minor or major)	3	Put in damp newspaper. Trailing habit for large bouquets.
Philodendron	1	Hothouse varieties desirable.
Photinia glabra	1	Some leaves have red coloring.
Pine	1	Use with other evergreens in winter designs. Use needlelike points to lighten.
Pittosporum	1	Roseate form. Variegated form desirable.
Plantain lily	2	See Hosta.
Pothos		
(Scindapsus)	1	Heart shape for accent.

Chart II 177

Foliage	*Wiring*	*Suggestions*
Rainlily		
(Zephyranthes)	1	Use tubelike leaves in a group.
Redwood	3	Evergreen sprigs for lightness.
Rhododendron	2	Broad, rich. Cut down.
Rhubarb	2	Young leaves best in form and color.
Rose	3	First choice with roses.
Rubber	2	Cut down. Yellowing leaves effective.
Salal	1	Long-lasting citrus-like foliage.
Scindapsus	1	See POTHOS.
Sansevieria	2	Cut down. Bold, tailored. Border is interesting.
Saxifrage	2	Delightful red tones in fall.
Screwpine	2	See PANDANUS.
Sea Grape	2	Dries brown. Excellent for hats.
Skimmia	1	Red in fall. Good substance.
Smilax	3	Fine foliage best. Southern smilax good for metallic painting. Use for trailing effect.
Spathyphyllum	2	Cut leaf to size. Charming with own blossom.
Stock	1	Plunge in water. Gray, soft, woolly.
Succulents	1	Experiment with many varieties.
Tradescantia		
(Wandering jew)	2 or 3	Wire large leaves individually. Reverse for purple leaves. Wire as for 3 when used as a trailing effect. Individually use #2.
Tulip	1	Rich blue-green. Cut to size. Tip good.
Viburnum	2	Cut down. Rare brown underleaf and heavy top veining. Fine with yellows and browns.
Vinca	3	See PERIWINKLE.
Violet	1	Put in damp newspaper for crispness.
Wandering jew	2 or 3	See TRADESCANTIA.
Yew	1	Dark green sprigs for winter decor.
Yucca	1	Reduce to size needed. Gray-green, swordlike. Use with modern designs.
Zephyranthes	1	See RAINLILY.

CHART III—CORSAGE BERRIES, SEED PODS, CONES, AND FRUITS

1	2	3
Wire up into cluster	Wire through lower fruit	Wire between lower scales of cone

4	5	6
Pierce solid seed pods and wire acorns	Wire stems of slender and lobed seed pods	Guide wire up into seed

Material	Wiring	Suggestions
Alder	5	Green cones and catkins. Excellent dried also.
Anise	1	Fine head. Good for painting.
Apple, lady	2	Tiny, decorative apples.
Ardisia	1	Long-lasting red berries.
Aucuba japonica	1	Berries of green, orange, and red.

178

CHART III   179

Material	Wiring	Suggestions
Australian pine		
(Casuarina)	5	Tiny cone. Very valuable.
Azalea (seed pods)	5	Delicate and light.
Bauhinia	5	Long twisted pod. Cut to size. Fine light-dark contrast.
Bayberry	1	Tiny gray berries close to twig. Aromatic.
Bittersweet	1	Orange to red. Exquisite form.
Blueberry	1	Rich gray-coated berries.
Camellia	5	Three-way seed pod.
Casuarina	5	See AUSTRALIAN PINE.
Cattail	5	Use miniature form.
Cedar	5	Leave cones on leaves.
Cinnamon	4	Use sticks in herb corsage, or for pointed color notes.
Crabapple	2	Use tiny apples.
Cranberrybush		
(Viburnum opulus,		
High cranberry)	1	Red cluster berries. Last through winter.
Cryptomeria	5	Small cone and foliage good together.
Daylily	4	Three-lobed pod. Great variety in shape.
Dogwood	1	White berries in clusters.
Duranta repens	1	Yellow pendant berries.
Elaeagnus pungens	1	Grayed apricot to magenta berries.
Eucalyptus	4	Many sizes, shapes, and colors.
Euonymus europaeus	1	Two-toned berries.
Filbert (with covering)	5	Hazelnut. Rare design.
Gladiolus	5	Three-lobed pod.
Grass	1 or 5	Grasses, oats, wheat, sea oats make distinctive notes in corsages.
Hawthorn	1	Cluster berries. Some last into spring.
Heather	1 or 5	Sprigs for lightness.
Hemlock	3	Tiny cones for contrast with large cones.
Holly	1	Many varieties. Holiday favorite.
Iris, Siberian	4	Beautiful slender seed pod.
Ivy	1	Green to purplish-black berries.
Jacaranda	4	Split open. Surprise markings inside. Pierce one half twice. Wire over stem of second half.

Material	Wiring	Suggestions
Jasmine, night blooming		
(Cestrum nocturnum)	1	White berries. Use with variegated
Juniper	5	holly or ivy.
		Blue berries with frosty covering. Use
Kumquat	2	with leaves.
		Tiny yellow-orange fruit. Push up guide
Larch	3	wire first, hook, then #2 wiring.
Lime	2	Cones slightly larger than hemlock.
Lipstick pods	5	Use the tiny immature fruit.
(Bixa orellana)		Hawaiian pods split and showing red
Liriope	1	berries. See Plate X.
Lotus	5	Black berries of excellent texture.
		Cornucopia shaped pods. Select small
Madrona	1	size.
Mountain ash	1	Dull red-brown berries.
Nandina	1	Large green, orange, and red berries.
		Use from green to red. Excellent keep-
Oak (acorns)	4	ing quality.
		Glue cap to nut with cement. Collect
Oleander	5	many varieties.
Orange, Calamondin	2	Long slender pods. Separate halves.
		Golden fruit. Small. Push up guide
		wire first, hook, and pull down.
Palm, coconut	5	Dried seed pod. Use the wavy stem also.
Pepper	6	Use when green, yellow, orange, and
		red.
Pepper tree		
(Schinus molle, California		
pepper)	1	Pink, red-violet berries.
Pepper tree		
(Terebinthifolia, Brazilian		
pepper)	1	Red berries.
Pernettya	1	Berries are white, orchid, and dubonnet.
Persimmon	5	Choose small fruits. Use just the calyx
		of hybrid persimmons.
Philippine Lily		
(L. philippinense, L.		
formosanum)	4	Separate pod into thirds. Fine line.
Pine	3	All varieties useful. Cut large cones into
		flowers or fashion flowers from indi-
		vidual scales.

CHART III 181

Material	Wiring	Suggestions
Poppy	5	All varieties have interesting pods.
Privet	1	Tiny black berries. Use green, too.
Pussy willow	6	Gray to pink. Many shapes. Use with broadleaf evergreen foliage.
Pyracantha	1	Orange and red berries.
Raphiolepis	1	Dull, rich black berries.
Rhododendron	5	Star-like clusters.
Rose (hips)	5	Allow calyx to remain. Distinctive.
Skimmia	1	Green and red berries, long-lasting.
Snowberry	1	White, waxy. Coat with preservative or warm paraffin.
Spruce	3	Perfectly designed scales. Cut large cones into cone flowers.
Sweet gum	5	Round balls with holes.
Sycamore	5	Balls have pebbly texture. Choose small ones.
Tuliptree	5	Long pointed pods. Paint with shellac to prevent shattering.
Viburnum	1	Berries in variety.
Wistaria	5	Long gray suede pods. Cut to size.
Wood roses (Ipomoea tuberosa)	4	Extreme longevity.
Wood cherries (Argyreia nervosa)	5	Similar to wood roses, though smaller. Gray suede sepals, brown center. Also known as miniature wood roses.

INDEX